Racist, Not Racist, Antiracist

PHILOSOPHY OF RACE

Series Editor: George Yancy, Emory University

Editorial Board: Sybol Anderson, Barbara Applebaum, Alison Bailey, Chike Jeffers, Janine Jones, David Kim, Emily S. Lee, Zeus Leonardo, Falguni A. Sheth, Grant Silva

The Philosophy of Race book series publishes interdisciplinary projects that center upon the concept of race, a concept that continues to have very profound contemporary implications. Philosophers and other scholars, more generally, are strongly encouraged to submit book projects that seriously address race and the process of racialization as a deeply embodied, existential, political, social, and historical phenomenon. The series is open to examine monographs, edited collections, and revised dissertations that critically engage the concept of race from multiple perspectives: sociopolitical, feminist, existential, phenomenological, theological, and historical.

Recent Titles in the Series

Racist, Not Racist, Antiracist: Language and the Dynamic Disaster of American Racism, by Leland Harper and Jennifer Kling

Ontological Branding: Power, Privilege, and White Supremacy in a Colorblind World, by Bonard Iván Molina García

Black Men from Behind the Veil: Ontological Interrogations, by George Yancy

White Educators Negotiating Complicity: Roadblocks Paved with Good Intentions, by Barbara Applebaum

White Ignorance and Complicit Responsibility: Transforming Collective Harm Beyond the Punishment Paradigm, by Eva Boodman

Iranian Identity, American Experience: Philosophical Reflections on Race, Rights, Capabilities, and Oppression, by Roksana Alavi

The Weight of Whiteness: A Feminist Engagement with Privilege, Race, and Ignorance, by Alison Bailey

The Logic of Racial Practice: Explorations in the Habituation of Racism, edited by Brock Bahler

Hip-Hop as Philosophical Text and Testimony: Can I Get a Witness?, by Lissa Skitolsky

The Blackness of Black: Key Concepts in Critical Discourse, by William David Hart

Self-Definition: A Philosophical Inquiry from the Global South and Global North, by Teodros Kiros

A Phenomenological Hermeneutic of Antiblack Racism in The Autobiography of Malcolm X, by David Polizzi

Buddhism and Whiteness, edited by George Yancy and Emily McRae

Racist, Not Racist, Antiracist

Language and the Dynamic Disaster of American Racism

Leland Harper and Jennifer Kling

LEXINGTON BOOKS
Lanham • Boulder • New York • London

Published by Lexington Books
An imprint of The Rowman & Littlefield Publishing Group, Inc.
4501 Forbes Boulevard, Suite 200, Lanham, Maryland 20706
www.rowman.com

86-90 Paul Street, London EC2A 4NE

Copyright © 2022 by The Rowman & Littlefield Publishing Group, Inc.

British Library Cataloguing in Publication Information Available

Library of Congress Cataloging-in-Publication Data

Names: Harper, Leland Royce, author. | Kling, Jennifer, 1984- author.
Title: Racist, not racist, antiracist : language and the dynamic disaster
    of American racism / Leland Harper and Jennifer Kling.
Description: Lanham : Lexington Books, [2023] | Series: Philosophy of race
    | Includes bibliographical references and index. | Summary: "This book
    unearths and outlines the semantic foundations of white fragility and
    their consequences for racial justice in the United States. It argues
    that by expanding our racial vocabulary in certain ways, we can make
    progress toward justice equally enjoyed by all"— Provided by publisher.
Identifiers: LCCN 2022029554 (print) | LCCN 2022029555 (ebook) | ISBN
    9781793640420 (cloth) | ISBN 9781793640437 (epub)
Subjects: LCSH: Racism—United States. | Racism in language—United States.
    | United States—Race relations.
Classification: LCC E184.A1 H328 2023 (print) | LCC E184.A1 (ebook) | DDC
    305.800973—dc23/eng/20220802
LC record available at https://lccn.loc.gov/2022029554
LC ebook record available at https://lccn.loc.gov/2022029555

America has failed miserably to have a serious and honest engaging conversation about race, one for which the aims ought to be to heal this nation.

George Yancy, *Backlash* (2018)

Contents

Acknowledgments

Completing any book project, let alone a co-authored book project, often requires a lot of support from a number of different corners. Completing this book was no different. As the initial ideas for this book came out of an essay that we originally wrote for a special issue of *Res Philosophica*, we must thank the journal and the special editors of the Mass Incarceration and Racial Justice Issue, Scott Berman and Chad Flanders, for the initial opportunity to develop and present some of these ideas in 2020. Additionally, thanks to the editorial team at Lexington Books, who have supported our early careers.

Such a co-authored book would not be possible, especially during a global pandemic, were it not for some help with the logistics of being able to acquire the necessary research materials, hold virtual meetings, travel across the continent to meet face-to-face, and keep us both generally well nourished and somewhat energized throughout this entire process. Our thanks go out to the University of Colorado, Colorado Springs, the UCCS Heller Center for the Arts & Humanities, and Siena Heights University.

We would also like to thank all of our colleagues, students, anonymous reviewers, and Concerned Philosophers for Peace, for allowing us to share our ideas with you and for providing us with much needed feedback, suggestions, and guidance. We also both share a deep gratitude for our research assistant, Romello Valentine, who went above and beyond not only in helping with our research but also in contributing valuable insights and ideas during our thinking and writing sessions.

Last, but certainly not least, we would like to thank our partners and children for providing us the mental and physical time and space to carry out this work. Thank you, Patrick, Marina, Kaylee, Emmeline, and Beau for your support and understanding. Now that we are done with this, you can each have your partners and parents back—until the next project.

This book is dedicated to all those who are working to make this world more equitable, inclusive, and just. We hope this book helps to light the way.

Land Acknowledgment

Acknowledging that we completed this book project on the unceded home-lands of Indigenous peoples is an important step in recognizing the history and the original stewards of these lands. We are privileged to have had this opportunity as part of our ongoing pursuit of knowledge and it is important that each of us acknowledge and reflect on that privilege, what it means, and how we can use it to create positive change.

Preface

For most white people, the worst thing to be called is "racist." We become downright irrational in the face of this charge, claiming to have been falsely accused of something akin to murder.

—Robin DiAngelo[1]

In 2019, US Senate Majority Leader Mitch McConnell said, among other things, that paying reparations for American slavery was not a good idea because the country had previously elected an African American president. McConnell's comments elicited, from us (two academic philosophers), two questions: "is he that stupid or is he that racist?" and ". . . and is there a meaningful distinction between the two?" To be sure, racism does not equate to stupidity and stupidity does not equate to racism—but the simple fact is that we did not have the correct terminology that we needed to describe the situation in the way in which we wanted to describe it. How should we regard McConnell's race-based comments? (Bearing in mind Hanlon's razor, also sometimes called the "devil theory" fallacy, which states, "never attribute to malice [or villainy] that which is adequately explained by stupidity.")[2]

Thinking on the distinction between stupidity and racism, considerations related to responsibility, and the role that language plays in how we contextualize and communicate about race-based situations, led us to co-author an essay addressing some of these theoretical ideas and their practical consequences. This essay, which is the foundation for chapter two and, ultimately, this entire project, is titled "The Semantic Foundations of White Fragility and the Consequences for Justice" and was published in *Res Philosophica* as part of a 2020 special issue on the topic of Mass Incarceration and Racial Justice.

Given the space constraints that come with publishing a peer-reviewed essay, we were unable to consider in full detail the various issues at play. The next natural step was to expand our thinking into a full-length book. As such, over the next eighteen months, through the course of a global pandemic, we read a lot, presented at conferences and workshops, spoke to colleagues and students, and ultimately put together this book. It connects theoretical considerations with real-life, concrete consequences and offers one tangible solution (among others).

This book splits the difference between Ijeoma Oluo's *So You Want to Talk About Race* and Charles Mills's *The Racial Contract*, with a little bit of Carol Anderson's *White Rage* thrown in for good measure. It contains arguments in philosophy of language, metaphysics, political obligation, ethics, and the pragmatics of political action. As an exercise in practical philosophy, it is unlikely to satisfy everyone. However, we regard it as essential to both provide a way forward, in the American context, for those who care about justice and give arguments for why our proposed semantic route is appropriate. It is not the only route, to be sure; but we do think it has so far been under-utilized in the fight against structural, antiBlack racism and for justice more equally enjoyed by all.

THE SPECIFICS

In chapter one, we begin by characterizing racism in the United States as an ongoing, dynamic disaster. Through discussions of the personal, inter-personal, institutional, and systemic aspects of American antiBlack racism, we demonstrate first that it is dynamic. It shifts its form, although not its function, over time. Then, pulling from Naomi Zack's recent work, we argue for framing racism as a disaster. By taking an in-depth look at 9/11 and Hurricane Katrina, we see that disasters demand institutional and interpersonal response. Our framing of racism as a dynamic disaster is both appropriate and helpful: it matches Naomi Zack's conceptualization of *disaster*, gives a straightforward reason and motivation for action at all levels of society, and, to some extent, explains why sufficient relief has not yet been provided. We conclude by introducing our proposed response to the dynamic disaster of racism: the semantic route. Although the semantic approach is surely only one response among many, we maintain that it is both appropriate and practical, as we go on to argue in subsequent chapters.

In chapter two, enlarging on Robin DiAngelo's work, we argue that an underlying cause of white fragility is an impoverished semantics of racism. The semantic false trinary of racist/not racist/antiracist does not allow for discussion of race-based situations in ways that do not immediately trigger white fragility. When describing race-based situations, the only options we have, linguistically speaking, divide those involved into good people (*not racist* or *antiracist*) and bad people (*racist*). This division often triggers white fragility, which leads to conversations being shut down before they can even start. Thus, racial injustice at both the interpersonal and institutional levels—which is the status quo—is maintained. This has serious consequences for justice: it perpetuates the mass incarceration of Black Americans and undergirds the knowledge gap and subsequent wealth gap. The result of these racial injustices, which are maintained partially through white fragility, is that Black Americans do not live in a democracy. The dynamic disaster of racism continues, helped along by the semantic false trinary. Our proposed solution: expand our semantics.

In chapter three, we focus on the COVID-19 pandemic. We argue that Black Americans are at far greater risk not only to contract the virus and suffer the associated symptoms up to and including death, but also to suffer long-term and generational setbacks in their efforts to improve their, and their communities', socioeconomic status. Regarding COVID-19, Black America is more susceptible to deeper, generational, defining losses than is white America. However, the semantic false trinary precludes fruitful conversations about this aspect of the dynamic disaster of racism and thus of potential solutions. It is unlikely that we can, at least in regular conversation, say that the COVID-19 pandemic or institutional and interpersonal responses to it are *racist, not racist*, or *antiracist*. Those terms simply do not fit. But because we cannot properly describe the institutional and interpersonal nature of these race-based problems in the conversations we have—and must have—about how to respond to this global pandemic at all levels of society, we are prevented from moving forward. The unjust status quo remains firmly in place.

In chapter four, we argue that taking up an expanded semantics of racism is a political obligation both for those who are concerned to make the United States a democracy and for those who care about justice more broadly. First, following W. E. B. Du Bois and Eddie S. Glaude Jr., we take up a conception of democracy that is conversation-oriented and community-based. To transform the United States into a Du Boisian democracy, we need to create conversational spaces where people can engage in difficult, productive dialogue about the nature of the race-based problems American society faces and potential solutions. For this to happen, an expanded semantics of racism is needed: we need a way to converse with others about race-based incidents without triggering their white fragility. Only then do we have a chance of achieving true democratic equality for all.

Second, following Iris Marion Young, we put forward a conception of justice that focuses on the social processes and practices that form the background conditions of our society, against which our interpersonal actions take place. These social processes and practices can either be oppressive and dominating, or liberatory and developmental—and when they are the former and not the latter, as they are in the contemporary United States, we have an obligation to change them, to bring about justice more equally enjoyed by all. To fulfill this political obligation, we need an expanded semantics of racism, that a) holds people accountable without blaming them and causing them to shut down and b) motivates them to act in concert with others to bring about justice. It is only by acting together that we can change the unjust social processes and practices of society; an expanded semantics will help us do that. In chapter five, we further the claim that people should care about justice.

In chapter six, we consider the dialogic constraints on communicating about racism in the contemporary United States. Assuming the goal is to motivate others to work together to bring about democratic communities and justice more equally enjoyed by all, people must attend to existing communicative contexts and structure their conversations accordingly. This means, at a minimum, that the conversational leaders ought to consider their audience's capacities, their own and others' well-being, and whether they are positioned in society such that they can have such conversations without serious risk of increasing their own or others' oppression. At the same time, their interlocutors must strive to sit in discomfort, to tarry with their race-based attitudes and actions and come to new and necessary recognitions about the dynamic disaster of racism in the United States. We conclude with a discussion of the political, interpersonal, and personal reasons for accepting the semantic expansion and dialogic constraints that we propose.

In chapter seven, we propose one term, *racial insensitivity*, to contribute to the expanded semantics of racism for which we call. Language is important to perception, attitudes, and actions. By considering a series of cases, we demonstrate that the term *racial insensitivity* both more accurately describes certain race-based incidents and situations, and enables us to call in the agents involved in those situations because it is less likely to trigger white fragility. Now so armed, we return to the Mitch McConnell case with which we began the Preface to provide our final analysis of his public commentary. We then consider some possible objections to our view. We conclude by outlining the criteria any proposed term must satisfy if it is to do the necessary work called for by our semantic approach, and invite others to join us in this needed semantic expansion.

NOTES

1. From *Nice Racism* by Robin DiAngelo. Copyright © 2021 by Robin DiAngelo. Reprinted by permission of Beacon Press, Boston.

2. Arthur Bloch, *Murphy's Law Book Two: More Reasons Why Things Go Wrong!* (Los Angeles: Price Stern Sloan, 1980), 52.

Chapter One

The Dynamic Disaster of Racism

George Bush doesn't care about Black people.

—Ye[1]

American antiBlack racism[2] is a truly dynamic phenomenon. Just as we have seen various mutations of the COVID-19 virus over the course of the pandemic during which this text is written, so too have we seen various mutations of racism over the past 400+ years. It has transitioned from chattel slavery, to Jim Crow segregation, to redlining, to the war on drugs, to mass incarceration, to unjust hiring practices, to police brutality, to voter suppression, to microaggressions and colorblindness. This list is neither exhaustive nor perfectly chronological; it is merely a representation of the ways in which racism has shown itself to be incredibly dynamic. This dynamic nature has rendered any would-be solutions short-lived, narrow in scope, or otherwise largely ineffective. Just as a remedy for a particular manifestation of racism is put into place, another iteration crops up elsewhere. It is a never-ending game of whack-a-mole with major domestic and global consequences—but the good news is that we have a lot of tokens left to play.

Before moving much further into the discussion it is important to say that we limit our scope to Black-white race relations in the contemporary United States unless otherwise indicated.[3] This is not to minimize the importance of other race relations between different groups, in different geographical locations, or in different eras, but to reflect that most of the relevant literature in philosophy of race centrally focuses on Black-white race relations in the United States. This is a lacuna in the field, but one that we cannot address here. One of us is Canadian and the other is American. As such, we choose to limit our scope accordingly. That is not to say, however, that what we argue

1

does not or cannot apply to other situations; quite the opposite, in fact, as we think that our conclusions can be applied—with some contextual and situational amendments—more broadly, to any number of race-based situations (Black-white or not).

The dynamic nature of racism has deeply felt individual, interpersonal, and systemic effects. For these effects, we can look first to a story shared by Martin Luther King, Jr., in his famous "Letter from Birmingham Jail." As he writes, racism is not only about constitutional rights and economic inequities; it is also about

> . . . when you suddenly find your tongue twisted and your speech stammering as you seek to explain to your six-year-old daughter why she cannot go to the public amusement park that has just been advertised on television, and see tears welling up in her little eyes when she is told that Funtown is closed to colored children, and see the depressing clouds of inferiority begin to form in her little mental sky, and see her begin to distort her little personality by unconsciously developing a bitterness toward white people; when you have to concoct an answer for a five-year-old son asking in agonizing pathos, "Daddy, why do white people treat colored people so mean?"[4]

Here, we see that the political is personal and the personal is political; they are intertwined, such that there is no sense to be made of separating them. Racism cannot be relegated to one arena—it affects, if not distorts, people's minds, bodies, and relationships, ultimately making them feel not at home in the United States.

Closer in time, we saw this when a colleague of ours, a Black, female academic and administrator, called campus security to report that the ceiling in her office had partially collapsed because of (we assume) a leaky pipe overhead. Upon arriving, campus security sternly told our colleague to leave the area because she was unauthorized to be there at the time—not knowing that it was, in fact, she who had placed the initial call. Campus security seemed disinterested in listening until at least one white person made herself present in the situation, thereby conferring legitimacy on the words of our Black, female colleague. Legitimacy on the words of our colleague who was not only the one who called to report the incident that occurred in *her* office but who is also a senior member of the leadership team at an institution of higher learning.[5]

Finally, recall when filmmaker, television host, MacArthur Fellow, one of *Time* Magazine's 1997 "25 Most Influential Americans," holder of 50+ honorary degrees, Harvard professor Henry Louis Gates, Jr. was arrested on suspicion of breaking into his own home in Cambridge, Massachusetts in 2009.[6] These particular examples demonstrate how Black Americans are made to feel unwelcome in particular spaces, places, and fields of work. This results in their underrepresentation in many arenas, making it less likely that the next generation of Black professionals will enter into various lines of work (because there is no representation). This is the cyclical nature of professional pigeon-holing—Black people are relegated to particular spheres, and because they are so relegated, it makes their absence from other spaces seem normal, acceptable, or deserved.

Part of the dynamic nature of racism is that it can be both explicit and implicit; while the examples we have cited strike us as explicit, there are no doubt some who would say certain aspects are implicit, and there are still other examples that we could cite where the racism is entirely implicit but still harmful.[7] Similarly, the harm caused by such racism can take many forms—it can be physical, economic, emotional, psychological, spiritual, and so on. Although the root of racism is the same, its manifestations vary with time, place, and context, and so too do its harmful effects. This contributes to difficulties with analyzing racism. While we do not provide a strict analysis of racism here, it is important to note that this dynamic aspect is an essential feature of it. Without recognizing this, it is tempting to see all of the cases we describe above as isolated incidents; but with the understanding that racism is dynamic, we can see them as being part of a whole, despite their differences, and despite the different harms they cause. (For the philosophers playing along at home, think about Socrates and his bees.)[8]

To properly assess and address racism, we must frame it correctly. This is precisely the task that Carol Anderson undertakes in the opening of her excellent book, *White Rage*—she tries to frame (and name) a race-based phenomenon that she and others are seeing and experiencing in the United States.[9] Although our framing is somewhat different than Anderson's, it's helpful to see that at a structural level, we're making a similar move. Correctly framing a problem is essential to finding a solution, because it serves to position our thinking and point us in the direction of potential solutions. Kenneth Cukier, Viktor Mayer-Schönberger, and Francis de Véricourt say that frames "enable us to generalize and make abstractions that apply to other situations. With them, we can handle new situations, rather than having to relearn everything from scratch."[10] Speaking particularly of Regina Barzilay and her role in utilizing artificial intelligence to aid in the discovery of antibiotics for treating drug-resistant diseases, they note that the correct frame was needed before a solution could be found. In discussing the standard approach to drug development, they point out that "conventional drug development mostly focuses on finding substances with molecular 'fingerprints' similar to ones that work. That generally performs well, but not for antibiotics. Most substances with similar compositions have already been examined, and new antibiotics are so close in structure to existing ones that bacteria quickly develop resistance to them, too."[11] Barzilay and her team, using artificial intelligence, shifted the focus from looking for structural similarities to focusing on the effect of whether the substance killed the bacteria. They go on to say that "Barzilay was a framer. By correctly framing the situation, she could unlock new solutions."[12]

Regina Barzilay and her team exemplify what can happen when a problem is correctly framed and then approached with appropriate intellect, care, and urgency. This is not to say, however, that all framing is correct framing. Cukier, Mayer-Schönberger, and de Véricourt remind us that "[m]isapplying frames can have horrendous consequences. In the 1930s the Soviet Union followed Lysenkoism, a theory of plant genetics. It was based on Marxist-Leninist ideology, not botany. Among its precepts was that crops can be planted close together because, according to communist theory, members of the same class live in solidarity and do not compete for resources."[13] Clearly, this instance of framing was unsuccessful and did not yield the intended results.

Properly framing a problem can drastically impact whether viable solutions are ever reached. So, how exactly should we frame the problem of racism? Given the dynamic nature of antiBlack racism, we contend that there is no one "correct" frame through which to view it. Reducing such a long-standing problem and all of its iterations to one perspective would seem at best simplistic and at worst counterproductive. There are multiple ways in which racism can be framed, and the ways in which it should be framed will be dependent on time, location, urgency, scale, and a whole host of other considerations. Given this, it is preferable to use as broad a framing as possible, which recognizes and takes account of the dynamic nature of racism without conflating distinct aspects that crop up in particular times and places. We thus propose one far-ranging frame—the disaster framing—without committing ourselves to the claim that it is either universalizable or uniquely correct.

FRAMING THINGS AS DISASTERS

In her 2021 book, *The American Tragedy of COVID-19: Social and Political Crises of 2020*, philosopher Naomi Zack discusses some of the common definitions of *disaster* as part of an attempt to see if and how the COVID-19 pandemic can be aptly termed a disaster.[14] The process that Zack uses to analyze COVID-19, we claim, is helpfully applied to racism because when something is declared, or framed as, a disaster, the approach to finding solutions for it changes.[15] When a disaster is declared, personal and institutional responses are demanded as a matter of necessity. So, it is worth taking a step back and thinking through whether it is appropriate to frame racism as a disaster, like Zack does for COVID-19. Spoilers, we think it is.

Of the classic definitions of disaster, Zack says "what we have is that a disaster is a destructive event, distinct in time and space, which is both physically and socially destructive, so that resources where it occurs are overwhelmed. Clearly, this won't do for COVID-19, which is global and, although it may have a beginning, does not have a foreseeable end."[16] While some aspects of the classic definition of disaster clearly apply to the COVID-19 pandemic, others do not. The same can be said for the classic definition of disaster when applied to racism—racism is physically and socially destructive, so that resources where it occurs may be overwhelmed but, as with COVID-19, it does not have a foreseeable end.

Adding a helpful idea to the classic definition of disaster to account for these (and other) shortcomings, Zack appeals to the work of E. L. Quarantelli, who has written extensively on the theoretical role of disasters. She writes:

> For Quarantelli, if changes in mental health accompany distinct events that would qualify as disasters, then those changes are part of the disaster. This idea merges what may have been viewed in cause and effect terms, with the disaster the cause and emotional depression an effect. Instead, according to Quarantelli, the emotional depression following the time of a destructive event, such as a fire or hurricane, is part of that disaster. This is what it means to say that disaster is *socially constructed*—certain changes in society should be viewed as part of a disaster and not merely an effect of a disaster.[17]

This slight but important change allows us to broaden the idea of what we consider a disaster. If what we might ordinarily consider the consequences of a disaster are part of the disaster itself, responses to the disaster necessarily include responses to those so-called consequences as well.

We can look at the events of September 11, 2001, as an example of what happens in response when a disaster occurs. At 8:46am EST, the hijacked American Airlines Flight 11 crashed into the North Tower of the World Trade Center. Seventeen minutes later, at 9:03am, a second hijacked plane, United Airlines Flight 175, crashed into the South Tower of the World Trade Center. This disaster rightfully demanded and elicited a number of responses. In the immediate vicinity, some people helped those who were running to safety, others blocked off streets to prevent people from getting any closer to the area and potentially putting themselves in danger, while still others, including civilians, police officers, firefighters, and paramedics, rushed to help the injured, and comforted not only loved ones but also complete strangers. There was widespread organization of public safety measures to coordinate rescue and recovery efforts, as people tried to learn as much as they could about what had just happened. At the highest level, the Federal Aviation Administration (FAA) shut down US airspace, the Federal Emergency Management Agency (FEMA) deployed to New York City and, later, then–US president George W. Bush and his administration began to make plans for military action.

The declaration of a disaster thus makes a difference to how we respond to things. If something isn't a disaster for you, or you don't see it as one, or it isn't so declared in your social and political context, you are far less likely to respond to it in urgent and perhaps essential ways. For co-author Leland, who at the time was a thirteen-year-old in Vancouver, initial reports about 9/11 didn't have an impact on him—he went back to sleep. By contrast, for co-author Jen, who at the time was a seventeen-year-old in Indianapolis, the live footage on her high school newsroom's TV led to classes being cancelled and a fundraiser being set up almost immediately. Both of our responses make sense, given our contexts; what we are drawing attention to here is that our alternative conceptions of it as "not-a-disaster" and as "a-disaster" rightfully changed how we each responded.

DISASTER RESPONSES

As a disaster, 9/11 demanded response at the personal, interpersonal, and structural levels. If we look at the individuals who were in and around the World Trade Center towers, the disaster began at approximately 8:46am and, for some of them, was short-lived because they were either killed or were rescued and recovered from any physical and mental trauma rather quickly. For policymakers and those charged with maintaining national security, we imagine that the disaster began shortly after 8:46am. Their disaster took place largely in the offices, hallways, and boardrooms of the buildings of Washington, DC, and consisted of assembling any available intelligence, assessing and dispatching resources, and more. It went on for, in some cases, decades.[18] For attorney Kenneth Feinberg and those working in his office, as was popularized in the 2020 Netflix film *Worth*, the disaster began over a year later as they were tasked with the unenviable job of administering the 9/11 Victim Compensation Fund.[19] And lastly, for the first responders that day we imagine that their disaster began shortly after 8:46am and likely continued for several days or weeks as they dealt with the physical and mental traumas of search, rescue, and recovery efforts. The disaster resurfaced for many of them years later through a host of health issues including, but not limited to, chronic rhinosinusitis, gastroesophageal reflux disease, cancer, and asthma that can be attributed to their work at or near Ground Zero.

The disaster of 9/11 has not been experienced by everybody, in the same place, at the same time, in the same way. Nevertheless, it is all the same disaster. How a disaster is felt and how it manifests itself can vary from individual to individual, from group to group, and can range over time and place. Accordingly, from the wide range of manifestations of this disaster, the responses to it, appropriately, have ranged widely as well. From immediate medical and mental health responses, to the creation, disbursement, and extension of the 9/11 Victim Compensation Fund, to enlisting and training more American and coalition troops to send to the Middle East in search of weapons of mass destruction (none of which were ever found), to increased security at airports around the world, the varied and dynamic nature of the 9/11 disaster necessitated varied and dynamic interpersonal and institutional responses. We are not saying all of these responses were or are morally correct; that is a further discussion. Our point here, rather, is that disasters demand responses at a variety of levels.

One specific response of note during the ongoing disaster of 9/11 was that provided by the residents of Gander, Newfoundland, Canada, in the hours immediately following the attack. As the FAA shut down all US airspace and grounded all planes, hundreds of flights needed to be immediately redirected to airports other than their original final destinations. One of the airports to which many flights were redirected was the Gander International Airport, located in Gander, Newfoundland, which is a town of approximately 11,000 residents. This airport landed more than 35 flights and more than 6,500 passengers, most of whom were stranded indefinitely. The response from many residents of Gander was to open their doors to these thousands of passengers, welcoming them into their homes, offering them meals, and providing them with necessities. In listening to interviews with Gander residents about their overwhelmingly welcoming response to the sudden (almost) doubling of the city's population in a matter of hours, the common thread that runs through their comments is that they felt a responsibility to help the stranded passengers—they *had* to do something to help.

For the residents of Gander, while they may not have been *directly* involved in the 9/11 disaster, at least not in the way that we typically speak of being directly involved with something, the 35+ flights and 6,500+ passengers coming into their community was part of that disaster. It was one that, for them, was unforeseen; it stretched resources beyond their capacities and demanded both institutional and interpersonal responses. The city of Gander established makeshift shelters, provided food, toiletries, and so forth. But, when the need wasn't met by these institutional responses, the citizens stepped up to bridge the gap. The response shown by the city of Gander and by its residents, throughout this disaster, was so successful that it inspired the Tony-nominated musical, "Come from Away." Many of the citizens and passengers are still friends to this day. This is a great example of how effective responses can be when an event is properly framed and the appropriate actions are subsequently taken at both the institutional and interpersonal levels.

Alternatively, when something is not framed or declared a disaster by a sufficient number of people (or by the necessary people), the demand for institutional and interpersonal response is not present, or at least is not present to the same degree as it would be were the event to be framed as a disaster.[20] Hurricane Katrina and the various responses to it (or lack thereof) serve as a good illustration of this point. An excerpt from a Britannica article, below, provides a slight sense of the considerations and the timelines associated with Hurricane Katrina after it caused tremendous damage in Louisiana in late August 2005. The article states:

New Orleans Mayor Ray Nagin had ordered a mandatory evacuation of the city the previous day, and an estimated 1.2 million people left ahead of the storm. However, tens of thousands of residents could not or would not leave. . . . As the already strained levee system continued to give way, the remaining residents of New Orleans were faced with a city that by August 30 was 80 percent underwater. Many local agencies found themselves unable to respond to the increasingly desperate situation, as their own headquarters and control centres were under 20 feet (6 metres) of water. With no relief in sight and in the absence of any organized effort to restore order, some neighbourhoods experienced substantial amounts of looting, and helicopters were used to rescue many people from rooftops in the flooded Ninth Ward.

On August 31, the first wave of evacuees arrived at the Red Cross shelter at the Houston Astrodome, some 350 miles (560 km) away from New Orleans, but tens of thousands remained in the city. By September 1, an estimated 30,000 people were seeking shelter under the damaged roof of the Superdome, and an additional 25,000 had gathered at the convention center. Shortages of food and potable water quickly became an issue, and daily temperatures reached 90°F (32°C). An absence of basic sanitation combined with the omnipresent bacteria-rich floodwaters to create a public health emergency. It was not until September 2 that an effective military presence was established in the city and National Guard troops mobilized to distribute food and water. The evacuation of hurricane victims continued, and crews began to rebuild the breached levees. On September 6, local police estimated that there were fewer than 10,000 residents left in New Orleans. As the recovery began, dozens of countries contributed funds and supplies [. . .] to assist with the cleanup and rebuilding. The US Army Corps of Engineers pumped the last of the floodwaters out of the city on October 11, 2005, some 43 days after Katrina made landfall. Ultimately, the storm caused more than $160 billion in damage, and the population of New Orleans fell by 29 percent between the fall of 2005 and 2011. . . . . A decade after the storm, the US Army Corps of Engineers acknowledged flaws in the construction of the city's levee and flood-protection system. In some parts of the city, levees and sea walls were not tall enough to hold back the water; in others floodgates did not close properly, and some structures collapsed entirely. Complicating matters was the fact that many parts of the New Orleans area vulnerable to flooding were not formally listed as flood zones by the Federal Emergency Management Agency (FEMA), so homeowners were not advised of their predicament, and they did not have flood insurance; both factors contributed to higher overall damage totals. Since then, New Orleans's flood-protection system was bolstered by $15 billion in federal funds, which were used to increase the heights of earthen berms and upgrade floodwalls and floodgates.[21]

As is evident, the Hurricane Katrina disaster lasted long after the storm itself ended. Katrina prompted varied responses, with various degrees of urgency. This is attributable, at least in part, to how this event was framed by individuals, groups, and institutions. In issuing the evacuation order, Mayor Nagin framed Katrina as a disaster and so demanded particular local institutional responses. By contrast, then–US president George W. Bush (who, incidentally, was also President at the start of the 9/11 disaster) did not declare Hurricane Katrina and its aftermath a disaster from the outset. This led to it being several days before an effective military presence and federal resources arrived on site. In failing to publicly frame Katrina as a disaster immediately and thus failing to quickly release federal disaster-relief funds and resources, it is as though Bush and his administration either were unaware of, or disinterested in, the unfolding damage to life and property. This prompted Ye to make the now-famous declaration (that appears as the epigraph of this chapter) that George Bush doesn't care about Black people. It is notable in this context that the population of New Orleans was 67.3 percent Black at the time.[22]

In comparison to the lack of immediate federal institutional response, the so-called Cajun Navy responded urgently to the obvious need for aid. Right after Katrina hit, former Louisiana state senator Nick Gautreaux put out a plea for help across local radio and TV. He asked for anyone with a boat who wanted to help the people of New Orleans to show up at Acadiana Mall in Lafayette, Louisiana. As journalist Trent Angers recalled, "They expected 24, 25 boats. Between 350 and 400 boats and people showed up."[23] The make-shift flotilla then made the two-hour ride from Lafayette to New Orleans, where they were initially blocked by local law enforcement, who told them not to enter the city. The rescuers launched anyways, ultimately rescuing over 10,000 people from flooded homes and rooftops before federal assistance arrived.[24] As rescuer Dave Spizale put it:

The spirit was I'm going to go help, I'm going to hitch it up . . . You saw people in New Orleans walking in chest-deep water with all of their possessions floating in a plastic garbage can, and you're looking at it and thinking this is in our country, and in our case, it's two hours down the road. So we were hard-pressed not to go into action. That's where we wanted to be.[25]

Clearly, the rescuers, who were later dubbed the Cajun Navy, framed Katrina as a disaster, and so viewed interpersonal and group action as a necessary response. This is evident from interviews with several rescuers, who simply said that going to help was the right, and obvious, thing to do. For them, it was imperative. As the Baton Rouge *Advocate* put it, "It was conscience, not a commanding officer, that summoned [the Cajun Navy] into treacherous currents to carry endangered citizens to higher ground."[26] We read this interpersonal response as being generated in part by the recognition, by these private citizens, that Hurricane Katrina was the start of a disaster, regardless of whether the US federal government declared it to be one. Such is the nature of disasters: they demand interpersonal, as well as institutional, response.

FRAMING RACISM AS A DISASTER

Earlier, we argued that racism is dynamic: it changes over time. Just when you think you've got a handle on it, it manifests differently, such that new tactics and strategies are needed to ameliorate and overcome it. In addition to being dynamic, we contend that American antiBlack racism can also be appropriately and helpfully framed as a disaster. Like 9/11 and Katrina, racism is physically and socially destructive, has overwhelmed community resources, and has changed society in indelible ways that can all be traced back to its origins in the seventeenth and eighteenth centuries.[27] To give one brief example, many crime-control tactics employed in modern policing in the United States originate in efforts by the first publicly funded police forces to "maintain public order."[28] At the time, this meant the silencing and removal of anyone regarded as dangerous by nineteenth-century businessmen, who largely controlled local politics. In the United States, that meant that predominantly Black (and also working-class) people and neighborhoods were targeted in a variety of ways by police. Given this history, it is no surprise that modern policing exacerbates tensions between police forces and the communities over which they watch.[29] Framing racism as a disaster makes sense of these kinds of societal changes *as racist*; rather than being merely the effects of racism, following Zack and Quarantelli, they are part and parcel of the disaster of racism itself.

American antiBlack racism can thus be appropriately viewed as a long, still-unfolding disaster. An unusually dynamic and large-scale disaster, but still, a disaster nonetheless. This framing, interestingly, matches some contemporary protest movements—both in the United States and globally—which have begun using slogans such as "Racism is a Pandemic" and "Racism is a Humanitarian Disaster." Some of this sloganeering, surely, is in an effort to keep activist spaces and movements focused on the "old" problem of racism as well as "new" problems such as COVID-19, climate change, and the ongoing refugee crisis. But we also think it reflects a growing understanding that racism is similar in kind and connected to these other things,[30] which are more commonly framed as, and declared to be, disasters.

Furthermore, when we frame racism in this way, we are able to see that it demands interpersonal and institutional response. This framing of racism is not only appropriate, then, but also helpful, in that it provides a straightforward reason and motivation for action. We must respond to racism at both the interpersonal and institutional level, because that is what you do when disaster strikes. The only question left—which is admittedly a difficult one—is how best to respond. What disaster relief should be provided? What solutions can and should be implemented? (You might also ask why relief has not yet been provided. As this chapter argues, we think it is at least partially because of a general failure, by either a sufficient number of people or the necessary people, to frame racism in this way.)

In the following chapters, we introduce one response to the dynamic disaster that is racism. We argue for a semantic shift in how we talk about race-based incidents and structural racism more broadly. Although it may seem modest, this response has the benefit of being both interpersonal and institutional. Anyone can do it, and if it is taken up broadly across American society, it is likely to lead to better institutional responses to racism as well. The semantic route for which we advocate addresses an insufficiency in the language that contemporary American culture uses to describe racism and its manifestations. This in turn creates conditions that enable people to recognize racism as a disaster and subsequently demands that they, and motivates them to, aid in its relief. Of course, our proposed semantic expansion is not the only solution; but as we contend in the remaining chapters, it is a viable one, and as the saying goes, any port in a storm.

NOTES

1. This is pulled from live video footage. See https://www.youtube.com/watch?v=ITuRPuhneAs.

2. Moving forward, we use the term "racism" to mean American antiBlack racism. There are numerous forms of racism, but this is our focus for this particular project.

3. The capitalization of "Black" and not "white" follows the current AP style guide, which recognizes that Black people, as opposed to white people, share a common experience of global historical oppression that makes such capitalization appropriate. For more, see David Bauder, "AP Says it Will Capitalize Black but Not White," *AP News*, July 20, 2020.

4. Martin Luther King Jr., "A Letter from Birmingham Jail," *The Atlantic Monthly* 212.2, August 1963, 2.

5. Incidentally and perhaps painfully ironically, this event occurred as we were holding a session to map out the ideas and arguments that we present in this book.

6. Then–US president Barack Obama famously called Gates' arrest "stupid," but never referred to it as racist. This points back to the original question which led us to develop our project, as presented in the Preface.

7. Thanks to Romello Valentine for pushing us to consider this point.

8. Plato, *Meno*, trans. Benjamin Jowett (Champaign, Ill: Project Gutenberg, 1990).

9. Carol Anderson, *White Rage: the unspoken truth of our racial divide* (New York: Bloomsbury USA, an imprint of Bloomsbury Publishing Plc, 2016).

10. Kenneth Cukier, Viktor Mayer-Schönberger and Francis de Véricourt, *Framers: Human Advantage in an Age of Technology and Turmoil* (New York: Dutton, 2021), 5.

11. Cukier, Mayer-Schönberger and de Véricourt, *Framers: Human Advantage in an Age of Technology and Turmoil*, 2.

12. Cukier, Mayer-Schönberger and de Véricourt, *Framers: Human Advantage in an Age of Technology and Turmoil*, 5.

13. Cukier, Mayer-Schönberger and de Véricourt, *Framers: Human Advantage in an Age of Technology and Turmoil*, 7.

14. Naomi Zack, *The American Tragedy of COVID-19: Social and Political Crises of 2020* (Lanham: Rowman & Littlefield, 2021).

15. While different language is used, this is similar to when Dr. King speaks of creating a *crisis* in his "Letter from Birmingham Jail." There, since little has been done to move the needle on US civil rights, Dr. King speaks of the need to create tension through direct action. This direct action will create a crisis (a financial one, in that particular case) which will ultimately demand some sort of response.

16. Zack, *The American Tragedy of COVID-19: Social and Political Crises of 2020*, 9.

17. Zack, *The American Tragedy of COVID-19: Social and Political Crises of 2020*, 9, emphasis in original.

18. We consider the twenty-year long war in Afghanistan and Iraq that was prompted by the events of 9/11 to be part of the disaster.

19. Sara Colangelo (dir.), *Worth*, MadRiver Pictures, Netflix, 2020.

20. Here, we here are thinking about declarations of disaster in the formal sense, where such a declaration is a necessary precursor to the garnering and release of institutional funds and resources. Framing something as a disaster is necessary for such

declarations, but not sufficient. Contrastingly, for interpersonal responses, framing is necessary and perhaps sufficient.

21. Editors of Encyclopaedia Britannica, "Hurricane Katrina," *Encyclopedia Britannica,* September 8, 2021.

22. https://www.census.gov/newsroom/facts-for-features/2015/cb15-ff16.html. As of 2014, which is the last year for which data is available, the Black population of New Orleans had declined by 7.5 percent, while the white population had increased by 4.7 percent. For those interested in issues of gentrification, this is a worrying component of disasters.

23. As quoted in David Begnaud, "How Citizens Turned into Saviors After Katrina Struck," *CBS News,* August 29, 2015.

24. Begnaud, "How Citizens Turned into Saviors After Katrina Struck."

25. As quoted in Begnaud, "How Citizens Turned into Saviors After Katrina Struck."

26. Walt Handelsman, "Our Views: Cajun Navy Rescues our Sense of Spirit," *The Advocate,* September 24, 2016.

27. A number of prominent thinkers have made the case that the modern concepts of race and racism get up and running in the seventeenth and eighteenth centuries. See, among others, Charles Mills, Kwame Anthony Appiah, Michelle Alexander, and Quayshawn Spencer.

28. Olivia B. Waxman, "How the U.S. Got its Police Force," *Time,* May 18, 2017.

29. Samuel Walker and Charles Katz, *The Police in America: An Introduction*, 8th ed. (New York: McGraw-Hill, 2012).

30. We use the admittedly non-specific "things" here because, following Zack, "events" seems much too narrow to capture the nature of the phenomena in question.

Chapter Two

The Semantic Foundations of White Fragility and the Consequences for Justice

*I was going to die, if not sooner then later, whether or not I had ever
    spoken myself.*
My silences had not protected me. Your silence will not protect you . . .
What are the words you do not yet have? What do you need to say?
*What are the tyrannies you swallow day by day and attempt to make your
    own, until you will sicken and die of them, still in silence? . . .*
*We have been socialized to respect fear more than our own needs for
    language.*

—Audre Lorde[1]

Discussion, judgment, or categorization of any situations that contain even a
hint of racial undertones, that many of us are likely to encounter in our daily
lives, is limited to a very narrow set of terms.[2] In assessing these race-based
situations, we are often forced to categorize them in one of two ways: racist
or not racist.[3] Having only these two categories available to us to describe
the broad spectrum of race-based situations is wholly inadequate and creates a false binary of how we are to assess, speak about, and ultimately form
beliefs about the current state of race-based situations.[4] The two terms, racist and not racist,[5] serve only to identify instances that appear at either end
of the continuum of race-based situations, failing to even acknowledge the
many situations that fall between them.[6] We argue here that the false binary
that is created by the limited vocabulary available for referencing race-based
situations has real, tangible consequences for racial justice, including the
creation and perpetuation of white fragility. This in turn perpetuates white
privilege, mass incarceration, the knowledge gap and related wealth gap, and
ultimately the circumvention of democracy for Black Americans. One possible way to make progress in the eradication of these injustices is to expand

15

the vocabulary available for use in describing race-based situations. A more robust semantic framework—one that does not perpetuate a false binary—is likely to reduce the frequency and severity of instances of white fragility, leading to more specific, accurate, and ultimately better conversations regarding race that can pave the way for positive social and political change.

FALSE BINARY

Some may be skeptical about the connection between semantics and real, practical change. The connection between theory and practice, in this particular case, is perhaps not evident; but we need not look far to see a plausible argument for it mounted in another arena. Ann J. Cahill,[7] in her discussion of Nicola Gavey's work,[8] discusses a distinction between *good* sexual interactions and *bad* sexual interactions, *permissible* sexual interactions and *impermissible* sexual interactions, *just* sexual interactions and *unjust* sexual interactions. She argues that none of these terms can suitably be applied to the bulk of our sexual interactions, and argues ". . . for the existence of a 'gray area' of sexual interactions that are ethically questionable without rising to the category of sexual assault."[9] Not only do Cahill and Gavey[10] argue that this "gray area" of sexual interaction exists, but also that this "gray area" is where the majority of our sexual interactions land, and that there is no proper term, or set of terms, with which to refer to them. There is no proper term to denote a sexual interaction that does not seem entirely right but that does not quite satisfy the criterion for sexual assault. Taking a moment to reflect on this, we can likely all imagine situations that fit this bill. One example cited by Cahill is that of a woman feeling pressure to engage in sexual intercourse with a man with whom she went on a date. This surely doesn't strike us as a sexual situation that is categorically right, nor does it strike us as a situation that we would consider sexual assault. There is a massive gap in the vocabulary—it only denotes the two extremes at either end of the spectrum, neglecting the majority of the instances on that spectrum. The available vocabulary is wholly insufficient to account for such a complex and diverse topic.

Borrowing from Cahill and Gavey, we argue that the semantic limitations present in discussions of sexual interactions also exist in discussions of race-based situations. Lacking the proper terminology, we are often unable to accurately describe race-based situations and express our relative feelings about those situations and so, for a variety of reasons that will be discussed in forthcoming sections, conversations about race are ended before they start.

The semantic options with which we are equipped to classify race-based situations are, in many cases, limited to two: *racist* or *not racist*. While, to be sure, not every situation that involves race needs to have an explicit categorization attached to it,[11] each of us subconsciously categorizes it at some point. If we think nothing of the situation, then it is likely that we thought it was not a racist situation, and so it is (at the very least implicitly) categorized by us as *not racist*. Similarly, if we thought that there was some heinous racially motivated unjust situation, then we categorize it as such: *racist*. The problem arises when we acknowledge the fact that the majority of everyday, mundane, race-based situations do not fit so neatly into either of these two boxes. But, since we only have two boxes, they must necessarily go into one of the two.

Perhaps an example may serve to best illustrate this point. Suppose a young, white family is preparing for a fun-filled Halloween evening. In their preparations, the six-year-old daughter puts on her costume that her parents purchased for her at a local big-box store; one which depicts (rather poorly) the ceremonial garb of a nondescript Indigenous tribe. Upon putting on her costume, her parents promptly send her out with her group of friends and a neighborhood parent to go trick-or-treating. Now, if we focus our attention strictly on the costume-wearing daughter, what exactly are we to make of this situation? How are we to react and, subsequently, categorize it? Surely this is a race-based situation that we need to categorize.[12] Given the two terms that are readily available to describe such a situation—*racist* and *not racist*—we may not be able to apply a term that sufficiently captures the complexity of the situation. This situation of a six-year-old white girl wearing a cheaply-made, mass-produced Indigenous garb costume does not appear to be *not racist*; there is clearly something racially unsettling going on here. But, most of us would likely refrain from calling this situation *racist* as well. This is, after all, just a young girl who put on a costume that her parents bought her and went out to go trick-or-treating with her friends. What this ultimately is, we would argue, is a race-based situation that clearly is not *not racist* but that does not seem to pass the threshold for being considered *racist*. This is an example of a race-based situation that falls within the "gray area" of the *racist–not racist* spectrum.[13]

To be fair, some will object to this example by noting that the problem is not with the spectrum itself, but with the lack of specification of what racism actually is. Once we have nailed down a specific working definition of racism, they might argue, we can apply it to this situation, and others, to see if they meet the requisite criteria for being considered racist. If they satisfy some minimal criteria, then they are racist, whereas if they do not satisfy the minimum criteria set out by that definition, then they are not racist. Our contention is that regardless of what definition of racism is adhered to, there will still always be the problem of race-based situations that do not quite meet the minimum threshold for *racist*, but that we do not want to call *good* or *advisable*, or even *generally acceptable*. Even if we want to reduce it to the simplest possible terms, living in an ideal world where we feel good about race-based situations that are not racist and we feel outrage about race-based situations that are racist, no matter what definition for racism is utilized, there will always remain a significant number of race-based situations that we do not quite feel good about, but that we also do not feel outraged about. Not having any proper terminology[14] to refer to these kinds of race-based situations creates a false binary, resulting in the idea that "if it does not create outrage, then it must be okay." This seems plainly wrong. Furthermore, this *racist–not racist* false binary serves as one of the foundations for, and perpetuates, what Robin DiAngelo calls *white fragility*, which we discuss later in this chapter.

FALSE TRINARY

Recently, the term "antiracist" has been successfully added to the race-based language lexicon. Presented perhaps most famously by Ibram X. Kendi in his 2019 book *How to Be an Antiracist*, Kendi uses this term to draw a distinction between passivity and activity in the fight against racism.[15] The uptake of this term allows us to plot another point on the *racist–not racist* continuum, ultimately demonstrating that "not racist" is more neutral than previously thought. While this is an invaluable addition to the lexicon, we still believe that there is more work to be done; more terms need to be added to account for the instances that are not plainly *racist*, *not racist*, or *antiracist*. As such, while in a better position than with the original false binary, this false trinary still leaves us with many of the same problems—we are insufficiently equipped to accurately describe the situations that we hope to describe and to properly contextualize the situations that we hope to contextualize.

One of the central problems that remains with the false trinary of race-based situation descriptors is that they are interpreted as being morally accusatory or character-aimed. While this is certainly appropriate in some situations, it may not be apt in each and every situation. What we are currently lacking, because of this false trinary, is one or more terms that explicitly are *not* morally accusatory and that explicitly are *not* character-aimed. Because of this false trinary, regardless of how these descriptors are intended, they are heard as moral condemnations and call outs to be a better person. Thus, they have a strong tendency to trigger white fragility.

WHITE FRAGILITY

In her 2018 book of the same name, Robin DiAngelo describes *white fragility* as an immediate defensive response, by white people, to any slight suggestion of the mere possibility that they are involved in something racist. Of white fragility, DiAngelo says, reflecting on some of her own experiences:

> It became clear that if I believed that only bad people who intended to hurt others because of race could ever do so, I would respond with outrage to any suggestion that I was involved in racism. Of course that belief would make me feel falsely accused of something terrible, and of course I would want to defend my character . . . I came to see that the way we are taught to define racism makes it virtually impossible for white people to understand it. Given our racial insulation, coupled with misinformation, any suggestion that we are complicit in racism is a kind of unwelcome and insulting shock to the system.[16]

The consequences of white fragility are not exhausted by the hurt feelings of individual white people; they expand well into the fabric of the American social order. Of the societal consequences that arise from white fragility, DiAngelo says

> . . . when we try to talk openly and honestly about race, white fragility quickly emerges as we are so often met with silence, defensiveness, argumentation, certitude, and other forms of pushback. These are not natural responses; they are social forces that prevent us from attaining the racial knowledge we need to engage more productively, and they function powerfully to hold the racial hierarchy in place. These forces include the ideologies of individualism and meritocracy, narrow and repetitive media representations of people of color, segregation in schools and neighborhoods, depictions of whiteness as the human ideal, truncated history, jokes and warnings, taboos on openly talking about race, and white solidarity.[17]

DiAngelo attributes white fragility to the fact that whiteness is invisible, due to its establishment as the cultural norm or standard. Because of this, white people have enjoyed the privilege of not constantly confronting issues regarding their race and, therefore, lack the requisite experience in discussing issues related to race without reacting in the ways described above. While we do not object to DiAngelo's proposed root cause of white fragility, we propose that another contributing factor is the false trinary that is created by the insufficient terminology available to describe race-based situations.

As is noted by DiAngelo, "[w]hites control all major institutions of society and set the policies and practices that others must live by."[18] When this undeniable position of social and political power is paired with the false trinary, it is easy to see how discussions of race can be and have been stifled before even starting. This is especially the case given that, as we mentioned above, attributions of racism are commonly viewed as extending from situations to persons; thus, to categorize a situation as *racist, not racist,* or *antiracist* is to implicitly categorize the relevant actor as a *racist person,* a *not racist person,* or an *antiracist person.*[19,20] The false trinary created by our insufficient terminology, then, not only blocks productive conversations about race-based situations, but also about race-based character attributes.[21] And having these conversations blocked means that white people remain inadequately prepared to engage in meaningful discussions about race.

To better draw out this connection, consider some of the potential reasons for why a Black person may not want to address a racial issue with a white person. Imagine Leland and Jen are co-workers in a predominantly white university philosophy department. Leland is a Black cisgender male professor and Jen is a white cisgender female professor and, while they are in the same department, they do not know each other very well, but enjoy a pleasant, respectable, professional relationship with one another. Suppose that, one day, Jen is having a conversation with some other faculty members about politics in her office and, while walking by, Leland overhears Jen say, as part of her conversation with the other faculty members, ". . . Leland must be very happy about the state commuting all of those marijuana sentences. I'm sure he has some friends or family who will get out of jail because of it." Having heard this, Leland has two general options: (1) confront Jen's comments in some as-yet undetermined way, or (2) remain silent and take no action. Which option should Leland take?

We do not propose to venture a prescriptive answer for what Leland should do here. To make, and defend, any such claim would take us too far afield from our current argument, which is firmly focused on delineating the semantic roots of white fragility and those roots' consequences for justice. What we do venture, however, is that in most situations Leland will opt for the latter option: he will opt to remain silent and take no action. Let us explore what his reasons might be.

(A quick note: when we use the term "categorize," it is meant to include the subsequent actions that align with that categorization. That is, for our purposes here, it is meaningless to say that a person categorizes a situation as *racist* but acts as if it is *not racist.* For the purposes of this book, which is focused primarily on the practical consequences of categorization, the subsequent actions of the categorizer dictate the situation's categorization.)

The option that presents the highest number of immediate or forthcoming negative consequences is the one in which Leland categorizes this situation as *racist,* confronts Jen's comments accordingly, and so ultimately creates what DiAngelo refers to as "disequilibrium in the habitus."[22] As an attempt to minimize the likelihood of creating this racial disequilibrium, Leland will often opt to categorize the situation as *not racist*.[23] Importantly, the negative consequences that would arise from Leland's categorization of the situation as *racist* would follow whether or not Leland was right in his categorization. On the one hand, if Leland is right in his assessment and Jen actually was making comments that, given the full context of the conversation, are racist, Leland's decision to confront her comments would likely result, at the very least, in strained relationships in the workplace. Very few people like to be confronted, either directly or indirectly, about doing something wrong even when they have knowingly done so. We have no reason to suspect that Jen would be any different in this regard. And moreover, her being accused of being a racist in particular (because that is what she will take from Leland's categorization of her comments as *racist*) is highly likely to bring her white fragility to the fore, which will likely result in her overreacting in the ways that DiAngelo describes. As such, Leland pursuing the matter and addressing it as a racist incident in the workplace would make for a difficult situation for him and at least one other co-worker. On the other hand, if Leland is wrong in his assessment of the situation and Jen's comments, given the full context of the conversation, are not racist, Leland's decision to confront her comments would most certainly result, at the very least, in strained relationships in the workplace. So, whether Leland is right or wrong is irrelevant because, if he categorizes the situation as *racist*, there is the very likely possibility that such a categorization will permanently negatively alter the landscape of relationships in his workplace.

Now, some may be curious as to why the maintenance of such relationships is so important, given that these relationships could potentially be with racists. Surely relationships with racists are not worth maintaining, especially not for a person who is a member of the group toward which that racism is directed. Here we must not forget that, as DiAngelo says, whites hold the power. As such, the status of Blacks' interpersonal relationships with whites has a causal relationship to other important aspects of their lives, such as health, wealth, justice, and so on. (We discuss these connections in more depth below.) White people in the United States have extreme influence over most, if not all, of the institutions that are crucial to Black Americans' well-being. That is the value of keeping these actual, and potential, interpersonal relationships with whites in good standing.[24]

For the Black man, the potential negative consequences of categorizing situations as *racist* are far greater than the negative consequences of categorizing them as *not racist*.[25] This is not to say, though, that there are no negative consequences that arise from categorizing the situation as *not racist*.

If Leland is not able to explain away, in his own mind, how he could have misconstrued Jen's comments as being racist when they really were not, then he faces an internal struggle that could have any number of psychological and emotional consequences. The argument here though, in line with DiAngelo's views about one of the causes of white fragility, is that the Black man has so much experience internalizing these kinds of struggles that he has the requisite ability to do so successfully. Just as the white person does not have the experience to be able to speak constructively about issues of race, the Black person has the experience to remain silent as a form of self- and (potentially, depending on the white person's particular amount of power, a form of) group-preservation.

For the Black person, when faced with race-based situations, because of the position of power that whites are in, he will often choose to categorize the situation as *not racist* in order to maintain the best possible standing of any actual or potential interpersonal relationships with whites as a form of self- and group-preservation. Categorizing these race-based situations as *not racist* and, in turn, not confronting them, only exacerbates what DiAngelo cites as the root cause of white fragility: whites lack the requisite experience to speak constructively about issues of race.

One way to disrupt the pervasiveness of silence and overreactions is to seek ways in which we can speak about race without eliciting the kinds of responses that DiAngelo outlines. In other words, one option is to find, or invent, the spectrum of language needed to broach the topic in a way that is less likely to overwhelmingly threaten the positive personal perception that whites have of themselves and their characters. We must amend and expand the vocabulary available to describe race-based situations, and adopt into our vocabulary toolbox some terminology that fosters personal growth, understanding, realization, learning, and improvement, rather than continue to utilize the same (false) trinary distinction that is so often tied to assessments of personal character, blame, and shame.[26]

IMPLICATIONS FOR JUSTICE

So far, we have argued that lacking the proper semantic resources to accurately describe our experiences of race-based situations results in a silencing of those who otherwise may be inclined to speak out about the negative consequences of those exact experiences.[27] Silence about the racial elements of particular experiences serves only to maintain and reinforce the status quo which, regarding the issue of race, has broad and deep implications for justice. This silence perpetuates white privilege, to the great benefit of those who hold it. The idea is that we cannot talk about race for fear of the negative consequences that occur when we are inevitably interpreted as making a character-based accusation of racism (which is, we have argued, what our current semantics both allows and encourages). But because we are unable to talk about it, those who benefit from racism either remain completely ignorant or in denial about it, or at the very least feel absolutely no pressure to alter either their own behavior or any of the structures of the society in which they live.[28] And this is based on the simple idea that "if nobody is talking about it, then there must not be a problem." The problem, however, is not that we do not want to talk about race, it is that we have been conditioned by society not to talk about race, because the only semantic resources we have available do not allow us to talk about race-based situations without calling the relevant agents racists. In short, it is partially for semantic reasons that we have been precluded from discussing race in any meaningful way that is socially acceptable.[29] And perhaps unsurprisingly, this semantic limitation manifests itself in the perpetuation of several linked systemic racial injustices in the United States.[30]

The first instance of a systemic racial injustice being partially undergirded by the semantic false trinary of racist/not racist/antiracist is the overrepresentation of Black people (Black men, specifically) in the United States' prison system. This is an aspect of American race relations that has been heavily focused on, and popularized by, Michelle Alexander's book *The New Jim Crow*. Alexander points out that the prison population in the United States is overwhelmingly Black while the overall population of the country is approximately only 12 percent Black.[31] The mass incarceration of Blacks is a systemic racial injustice, not only because the American criminal justice system is designed to create and maintain such mass incarceration, but also because the American prison system is deliberately trauma-inducing, which further victimizes Blacks insofar as serious trauma can lead to, and exacerbate existing, mental health issues such as PTSD.[32] This is a serious racial injustice that we cannot even hope to have a discussion about if DiAngelo's theory about white fragility, and our extension of it, is correct.

The mere suggestion that the country's mass incarceration problem is race-based is an idea that will be interpreted (because of the semantics of race) by many of those involved in building up and maintaining that incarceration structure, and the broader criminal justice system, as an accusation of them personally being racist and, more fundamentally, as an attack on their personal character. When Michelle Alexander (or someone, following Alexander) says, "the American criminal justice system is racist," what prison guard Bob, or jury member Susan, or police officer Mark, or law and order activist Catherine hears, is "you're a racist." Perhaps they should not hear this; perhaps they should. Our point, however, is that they *do* hear this, and it is, as philosopher Richard Rorty puts it in another context, "a conversation-stopper."[33] Once the accusation of character-based racism is heard (as it must be, if our analysis of the semantic false trinary surrounding race is correct), the possibility of constructive conversation about the racist aspects of the mass incarceration system is off the table. This is especially true when we remember that many of the people who have been and are currently in positions of power, the ones who make the decisions about the American criminal justice system, are white: they are precisely the people who are unlikely to be able to respond properly to racial discussions because, as DiAngelo puts it, they have not been trained to do so due to a lifetime of their race being invisible. Hence, the mass incarceration of Black Americans continues, with devastating effects (as we argue further below) for racial justice.

The second instance of a systemic racial injustice in the United States being supported by the (false) racist/not racist/antiracist trinary is the knowledge gap that persists between Black and white students. Derrick Darby and John L. Rury present a historical and philosophical account that explains some of the causes and consequences of the fact that "[k]ids vary in measures of educational achievement, but white students typically have better test scores than [B]lack ones, which is one familiar measure."[34] Darby and Rury attribute this persistent discrepancy between standardized test scores, subsequent admission into, and success in, post-secondary education and, ultimately, overall position in the American workforce and economy, to ". . . both inequality of educational opportunity and unequal social relations [that] were socially engineered and enforced with episodes of planned and spontaneous racial violence, the legal authority of state-sanctioned racial apartheid policy, and decades of local exclusion and discrimination based on color and other phenotypic characteristics."[35] In other words, the knowledge gap is the result of various racist policies, institutions, and actions, and the wealth gap between Blacks and whites in the United States is partially a result of that knowledge gap. (Of course, the wealth gap cannot be attributed solely to the knowledge gap; it is also partially attributable to American slavery and subsequent history, with the outright theft of Blacks' labor, land, and wealth, and the institutional blocking of Blacks' ability to pass their wealth on to their descendants.)

While Darby and Rury make a strong case for their argument, venturing this idea runs the same risks as are present with the above-noted topic of the overrepresentation of Blacks in America's prisons. The suggestion that statistical differences in education, employment, and wealth are race-based, and not simply merit-based, is to put forward a position that will be interpreted by many of those who are involved in, and supportive of, the United

States' education and economic systems, as an accusation of them personally being racist and, again, more fundamentally, as an attack on their personal characters and a denial of their own personal merits. Darby and Rury's basic argument is that the American education system, and the economic system it supports, are racist. Notice that any gloss of their argument must categorize these systems as *racist*, regardless of whether they themselves would prefer a more nuanced term, because the only two terms available in our common lexicon are *racist* and *not racist*.[36] Regardless, Darby and Rury are discussing systems; but what kindergarten teacher Pam, successful business owner Ken, and school principal Eric hear is, "your actions are racist, so you're a racist, and that means you're basically evil." At this point, their white fragility is likely to kick in, and the subsequent negative consequences that we outlined above are likely to occur. Thus, for the Black mom considering whether to confront her son's principal about his being placed into the lowest reading group without testing, it is strategically not worth it. The conversation is ended before it can begin. Hence, the knowledge gap continues, again with devastating effects for racial justice.

The mass incarceration of Blacks and the knowledge gap between white and Black students are, at least partially, perpetuated by the semantic false trinary of racist/not racist/antiracist. On their own, these are both instances of serious racial injustice in the United States, as many theorists have ably argued. However, we argue that, when they are put together, they serve as the foundation for yet another, perhaps even more serious, racial injustice: Black Americans do not live in a democracy. White Americans may or may not live in a democracy; much has been written in recent years about the American political system and its democratic and undemocratic aspects.[37] But if we consider one of the fundamental aspects of a democratic political system to be the potential for ordinary citizens to exercise, by right, some roughly equal measures of political control, or, at the very least, political impact, on collective political decision-making, then Black Americans do not live in a democracy.[38] In short, there are two political systems operating in the United States—one (potentially) democratic, the other authoritarian—and they are separated by a color line. And that political color line, also known as political white supremacy, is partially maintained by mass incarceration and the knowledge gap, which in turn are partially maintained by white fragility, which in turn is partially maintained by the semantic false trinary we identified above. Hence, it is all one dynamic disaster.

To see how the knowledge gap and mass incarceration result in Black Americans not living in a democracy, let us consider the political effects of each in turn. The knowledge gap is the result of generations of substandard education provided to Black families. It manifests itself in fewer Blacks completing secondary school, fewer Blacks attending and completing post-secondary education, fewer Blacks starting at or moving into senior positions in the workforce and, ultimately, fewer Blacks having the opportunity to accumulate any wealth. Because of the socioeconomic station that the Black American community as a whole finds itself in, partially as a result of lacking access to proper education, Blacks scarcely have the opportunity to occupy any positions of real power.[39] When we speak of positions of real power, we mean those positions that get to make substantial social and political decisions, be they in the workplace, the community, in legislation, or elsewhere. One study of sixteen Fortune 500 companies states that Blacks are underrepresented in senior leadership roles, when compared to the demographics of the overall employed workforce, by 13 percentage points.[40] As recently as late 2017 there were only four (set to be reduced to three because of the pending retirement of American Express CEO Ken Chenault) Black CEOs in Fortune 500 companies.[41] Similarly, the 116th Congress, which has been touted as the most diverse Congress ever, contains fifty-five Blacks, which amounts to roughly only 10 percent of the legislature.[42] Not only do Blacks often not have realistic opportunities to occupy these seats of power, because of their socioeconomic station, they also do not often have the ability to be present, even tangentially, in the halls of power. They are excluded from the conversation altogether; relegated to the workshop floor while the board meeting unfolds upstairs with no opportunity to have a meaningful say in the matters that are crucial to their own livelihood and well-being.[43]

Moreover, the knowledge gap manifests itself not only in fewer Blacks being afforded the opportunity to occupy positions of real social and political power, but also in fewer Blacks occupying the sorts of white-collar jobs that would allow them to at least attempt to engage in political discourse with those—as we have seen, predominantly whites—who do occupy positions of real power. Traditionally, white-collar, that is, salaried, positions allow workers time off to vote, to go to town meetings, to call or visit their congresspersons, or to engage in other standard acts of political discourse and protest. By contrast, blue-collar, that is, hourly, positions, do not tend to afford workers the freedom they would need to even potentially exercise their supposed rights, as citizens living in a purportedly democratic system, to various kinds of standard political engagement. And as Darby and Rury argue, the knowledge gap and subsequent wealth gap funnel Black Americans toward blue-collar jobs.[44] Thus, the Black American community's socioeconomic station, considered as a whole, not only precludes access to positions of real power, but also precludes the potential exercise of their supposed rights to engage in various political activities. And if there is no real possibility of exercising one's supposed democratic rights without penalty, it is difficult to say that one has those rights at all.

We now turn back to the mass incarceration of Blacks and its political effects. The American criminal justice system currently punishes individuals convicted of crimes with sentences that extend far beyond the prison cell. Michelle Alexander writes that "[o]nce you're labelled a felon, the old forms of discrimination—employment discrimination, housing discrimination, denial of the right to vote, and exclusion from jury service—are all suddenly legal. As a criminal, you have scarcely more rights, and arguably less respect, than a [B]lack man living in Alabama at the height of Jim Crow."[45] Given Alexander's remarks, especially as they relate to being denied the ability to vote or hold office, and the above-mentioned difficulties in achieving upward socioeconomic mobility, it is far more likely that Blacks will not and cannot sit in the seats of power or even hope to occupy the hallways in which the most crucial decisions of our society are made. Furthermore, they are often precluded from even having any direct input in electing those individuals who will occupy the seats of political power. In short, there are literally millions of Black Americans who either are locked up, or who have been locked up, and as a result have no ability either to move into the positions of power that decide their own fates and the fates of their communities, or to directly influence who comes to occupy those positions of power.[46]

This lack of political power is further compounded by the wealth gap. In general, Blacks are less likely to be able to afford to hire an attorney to get minor infractions expunged from their criminal records, whereas whites in general have the monetary power to do so. So while a criminal conviction is unlikely to permanently exclude a white person from the potential exercise of roughly equal measures of political control or impact, it is likely to permanently exclude a Black person. This, in concert with the disproportionate overrepresentation of Blacks that are subject to the criminal justice system as compared to whites, leads us to conclude that, while white Americans may live in a democracy, Black Americans do not. Blacks are precluded, by the institutionalized political effects of mass incarceration, the knowledge gap, and the wealth gap, from participating in at least two fundamental components of democracy: holding office and voting for who holds office. Put in more general terms, they do not have the potential to exercise any roughly equal measures of political control or impact. Thus, Black Americans do not live in a democracy; rather, they live in an authoritarian political system, where they are managed by the political instruments of the state rather than consulted about the creation, shape, and ongoing power of those instruments. This further racial injustice stems purely from historical and contemporary racist practices in America, which themselves are (at least partially) perpetuated by a fundamental inability to speak effectively about them with whites, in the hopes of righting some of the wrongs that have been, and continue to be, inflicted on the Black community.[47]

THE NEED FOR SEMANTIC CHANGE

Our analysis of the semantic foundations of white fragility and privilege, and its ultimate consequences for racial justice, suggests the urgent need for semantic change. Of course, changing the semantics that surround race-based situations is not a cure-all, and we do not put it forward as such. However, we do maintain that we cannot hope to change the minds of those who hold the power, and to educate them about the dynamic disaster of American racism, if we do not have the semantic tools to do so. The tools we currently have are insufficient to the task at hand; so, we must add some more to our toolbox. We need to add some new vocabulary and terminology to allow us to have free and open conversations about race without fear of activating white fragility and having the conversation shut down before it even starts. It is only when we have a set of terms that allows us to speak about these difficult topics without triggering immediate responses of fear, personal attack, accusation, guilt, and the desire to disengage that we will be able to garner widespread acknowledgement of ubiquitous racial injustices throughout the United States, and begin working toward a solution or set of solutions.

Of course, a quick response here might be that we do not need to introduce new terms to help whites be more comfortable discussing racism, but that we should instead prescribe to whites that they buck up and stop being so fragile.[48] While this approach is no doubt both satisfying and correct so far as it goes, it has the downside of not being particularly effective, or at least, not as effective as we might hope. Insofar as the goal is to rectify or even ameliorate the dynamic disaster of racism, there is no harm in adding any additional tools we can find to the toolbox. Our claim is not that re-working the terminology is the only way to accomplish anything, but rather that it is a viable way to address at least some instances of white fragility, and that is probably worth doing, given how white fragility strongly undergirds and perpetuates racial injustice.[49]

To see how changing our terminology might help address white fragility, consider kids: when they get in trouble and are overtly accused of doing something wrong, problematic, or against the rules, their immediate reaction is often defensiveness. However, when they are instead approached empathetically, with language approximating "listen, I know you didn't mean for this to happen . . ." or "I know this wasn't your fault . . ." they are more likely to respond with openness and a willingness to work together to rectify the relevant situation. We are not child psychologists; nevertheless, there is undoubtedly something to this approach.[50] And in a sense, if we take DiAngelo's argument to its logical conclusion, whites are similar to children in that they lack the requisite experience that would enable them to respond appropriately to race-based trouble. So, like we do with children, we should figure out how to linguistically scaffold our conversations with whites about race in order to help them along. We are certainly not advocating treating white adults like children; but opening up and broadening our semantic tool-box in these kinds of ways is likely to help diffuse white fragility and so make progress toward positive social and political change.[51]

In other words, we must adopt new, additional terminology regarding race, that goes beyond the false trinary of racist/not racist/antiracist, because doing so will allow us to speak about race-based situations and injustices without the immediate perception that we are engaging in personal attacks. And this has the potential to enable us to work collectively toward a common set of antiracist solutions. At first glance, this is a consequentialist argument for semantic change, and we are happy to make that consequentialist argument (although there is also a deontological argument to be made). Thinking from a consequentialist perspective, regardless of whether it is true that systemic racial injustices are existing white people's fault,[52] we will move faster toward justice, or at least positive social and political change, if we treat whites like partners in solution-finding rather than as at fault and to blame. This approach takes white fragility as a given, and attempts to work around it rather than through it in order to make political progress. Importantly, this is not to say that we should "baby" racists, or ignore overtly racist situations; rather, it is to say that opening up our semantics in order to facilitate more constructive discussions about race cannot hurt, and may well help. And anything that might help is worth doing, given that racial injustice in the United States is literally a matter of life and death.[53]

It is worth noting as well that, while adopting a more open semantics about race-based situations is likely to have good consequences, that is not the only reason for doing so. To start, it would enable us to more accurately describe the world; as we note above, there are gray areas between *racist* and *not racist*, and *not racist* and *antiracist*. A more open semantics would better reflect the situations and contexts in which we find ourselves. Additionally, much work has been done in recent years on responsibility and blameworthiness for collective wrongdoing, and apart from methodological individualists, many theorists have argued that individuals, while partially responsible—in the sense of being liable—for systemic racial injustices, are not fully responsible or all equally blameworthy.[54] Adopting new terminology in regard to race-based situations, then, not only has good consequences, but also more precisely reflects the complicated social and political world in which we live.

At this point, one objection might be that the racial injustices that we have identified as predicated on and upheld by white fragility are inherent to the United States, and so it is not worth working with whites within the system to fix them. We should be advocating for revolution, not for semantic changes that might encourage whites to fix some small instances of racism, but that will not, in the end, get rid of the dyed-in-the-wool white supremacy at work. Is the United States worth trying to fix?[55] We are not sure; however, we do think that the semantic changes we advocate are necessary regardless. If the United States is worth fixing—that is, if the existing political white supremacy can be eradicated—then semantic openness in regard to race-based situations will help, as we have argued, with that project. And if the United States is not worth fixing, then any revolution that is truly justice-oriented will need to embrace the semantic changes that we have discussed, because any revolution that does not do so will inevitably develop the same problems that we identify in this book, for exactly the same reasons. So, regardless of whether internal political change, or wholesale revolution, is what is needed to rectify systemic racial injustice in the United States, the semantic openness that we advocate will be a necessary component of the success of either enterprise.

SEMANTIC CHANGE AS ONE AVENUE FOR POLITICAL CHANGE

Ultimately, our goal is to offer a constructive solution to the dynamic disaster that is racism. Currently, the semantic tools that we have (the false trinary of racist/not racist/antiracist) and the approaches that we are utilizing (white people, stop being so damn fragile!) are not working as well as (we assume) many might hope. Those whites with the power to dismantle systemic racial injustices are practically incapable of seeing them as such, given the semantic and experiential foundations, and hence continued strength, of white fragility. Through the semantic expansion that we offer, the hope is that white America will become able to shift their view of American institutions. Not likely, perhaps, but possible. And the move from "practically impossible" to "possible, albeit unlikely," while small, would be a win that should not be discounted.

Perhaps it is simply academic wishful thinking that rationality will always prevail. It surely does not, and yet, we can hope. Again, our point here is not that we should "hedge" every accusation of racism, or refuse to call a racist a racist; rather, it is that we should be prepared for such accusations and call-outs to fail to garner the desired outcome, and so should have other semantic weapons in our arsenal to fight for democracy and racial justice.[56] So, we offer another avenue (one among what is surely many) for how we might go about facilitating more productive discussions about race, which hopefully will lead to more positive social and political action and change and, eventually, justice that is equally enjoyed by all.

NOTES

1. From SISTER OUTSIDER by Audre Lorde—published by Crossing Press, Copyright © 1984, 2007 by Audre Lorde. Used herein by permission of the Charlotte Sheedy Literary Agency.

2. This chapter was originally published as a journal article, "The Semantic Foundations of White Fragility and the Consequences for Justice," *Res Philosophica* 97 no. 2 (2020): 325–44. Our thanks to the journal for permitting us to republish it here with alterations.

3. There is the broader categorization "microaggression" that is sometimes used to describe these situations; however, that is not a sufficient term either, because it generally either connotes "racist," or is used more broadly to refer to any kind of one-off oppressive act (rather than specifically being used to call out race-based situations).

4. In a previous version of this chapter, we referred to this as a false dichotomy. We now feel that referring to it as a false binary is more accurate.

5. Sometimes, people say "non-racist" rather than "not racist." We regard these as equivalent.

6. The locution "a little bit racist" is becoming more common; however, notice that this phrase does not solve the problem we identify, insofar as it still categorizes situations as *racist* or *not racist*. Even though it works to soften the binary, it still reinforces its existence, and so is not an appropriate way of creating more constructive dialogues about race-based situations. Thanks to Kiran Bhardwaj for raising this point.

7. Ann J. Cahill, "Unjust Sex Vs Rape," *Hypatia* 31, no. 4 (2016): 746–61.

8. Nicola Gavey, *Just Sex?: The Cultural Scaffolding of Rape* (New York: Routledge, 2005), 2–3.

9. Cahill, "Unjust Sex Vs Rape," 746.

10. Gavey also addresses this, in more depth, in *Just Sex?: The Cultural Scaffolding of Rape*, Chapters 4–5.

11. That is, we need not make our categorization public in any way.

12. We are aware of the cultural implications but, at least in this particular example, the race component can be reasonably emphasized as well.

13. A sufficiently informed academic working in philosophy of race or associated areas might, following Lawrence Blum, refer to this situation as a *racial ill*. Lawrence Blum, "Varieties of Racial Ills," in *"I'm Not a Racist, but . . .": The Moral Quandary of Race* (New York: Cornell University Press, 2002), 53–77. However, it is worth

noting that neither this term, nor any similar terms introduced in the academic literature in this area, have received popular uptake. It also seems somewhat too strong to
refer to this situation as a racial ill, given the term's connotation of the perpetrator/s
of illness as germs, bacteria, or viruses. Is that really what we want to call the girl, or
her parents, in this situation?

14. Here it is not yet our aim to establish just what the proper terminology should
be. For that argument, see chapter seven.

15. Ibram X. Kendi, *How to be an Antiracist*, First ed. (New York: One World,
2019).

16. Robin DiAngelo, *White Fragility: Why It's so Hard for White People to Talk
about Racism* (Boston: Beacon Press Books, 2018), 4.

17. DiAngelo, *White Fragility: Why It's so Hard for White People to Talk about
Racism*, 8.

18. DiAngelo, *White Fragility: Why It's so Hard for White People to Talk about
Racism*, 27.

19. In this way, it is similar to bullying. Like *racist*, *bullying* often transfers from
being a description of the situation to being a description of the person acting in the
situation. So, although bullying does not have the power relations link that racist has,
this is a helpful analogy insofar as the term "bully" operates similarly to the term
"racist."

20. Interestingly, this is so despite many attempts by philosophers of race to define
racism in other more reasonable ways, such that the attribution of racism need not
extend straightforwardly from situations or institutions to individual persons. However, these academics' work has not received popular uptake, probably for a variety of
reasons, including that it is often difficult to disseminate abstract philosophical ideas
to the public, and that philosophers of race are likely to suffer epistemic injustice.
Furthermore, it is likely that this lack of uptake has something to do with white control of our popular semantic systems, as well; if racism can be made into something
that only horrible people engage in, then that is another way to bury constructive
discussion of it.

21. For example, a race-based character attribute might include racial disregard,
racial antipathy, or racial neutrality. J. L. A. Garcia, "The Heart of Racism," *Journal
of Social Philosophy* 27, no. 1 (1996): 9–17.

22. DiAngelo applies the term "disequilibrium" to Pierre Bourdieu's concept of
"habitus," which is the result of repeated actions, social dispositions and the like, as a
result of socialization. DiAngelo, *White Fragility: Why It's so Hard for White People
to Talk about Racism*, 108; Pierre Bourdieu, *The Field of Cultural Production: Essays
on Art and Literature*, ed. Randal Johnson (New York: Columbia University Press,
1993): 162–75.

23. Bearing in mind that *antiracist* is still an available option, though it clearly is
not applicable in this case.

24. There is an interesting discussion to be had here about how particular interpersonal relationships between Blacks and whites influence the white-controlled institutions that are essential to Blacks' well-being. We go into this in more detail below.

25. This is especially the case if we look at these as isolated incidences, as we are often forced to do.

26. Someone might respond here that expanding our vocabulary in such a nuanced way is simply not feasible, because many people just don't have the ability to speak in nuanced ways about such complex situations and topics. We have two responses to this worry. First, the existence of a variety of semantic arenas wherein nuance is both evident and celebrated belies this concern to some extent; consider how nuanced our vocabulary is around the evaluation of sports, food, and art, just to name a few. Second, to assert that people cannot take up more nuanced vocabulary ignores the rise of the LGBTQ+ movement, which in fifty years has gone from socially anathema to so commonplace that students regularly correct their professors' use of terminology and language to be both more precise and more complex. This suggests that while widespread adoption of an expanded semantics takes time, it is certainly possible. Thanks to an anonymous reviewer for raising this point.

27. Miranda Fricker and others refer to this phenomenon as testimonial injustice or testimonial smothering. See, among others, Miranda Fricker, *Epistemic Injustice: Power and the Ethics of Knowing* (Oxford: Oxford University Press, 2007); Rachel McKinnon, "Epistemic Injustice," *Philosophy Compass* 11, no. 8 (2016): 437–46.

28. This can be exemplified by Mitch McConnell's comments claiming that reparations for slavery are not necessary, or even a good idea, because a Black president had been elected. See the Preface for more on this case.

29. Of course, the limitations of our popular semantics around race-based situations do not, in principle, preclude people from *thinking* deeply, complexly, and meaningfully about those situations; but they do limit our ability to communicate our thoughts to others, particularly whites, without triggering white fragility.

30. This is a classic double bind, of the kind described by Marilyn Frye. Marilyn Frye, "Oppression," in *The Politics of Reality* (New York: Crossing Press, 1983), 1–16. If we talk about race, we are penalized, because the false trinary of racist/not racist/antiracist triggers white fragility. If we do not talk about race, systemic injustice and oppression continues to be the norm for Black Americans. This thus places racial semantics squarely in the political realm, as well as the ethical realm.

31. Michelle Alexander, *The New Jim Crow: Mass Incarceration in the Age of Colorblindness* (New York: The New Press, 2012).

32. Steven Swartzer, "Traumatic Incarceration." Unpublished Paper. Presented at RoME XII: Boulder, CO, 2019.

33. Richard Rorty, "Religion as Conversation-Stopper," *Common Knowledge* 3, no. 1 (1994): 1–6.

34. Derrick Darby and John L. Rury, *The Color of Mind: Why the Origins of the Achievement Gap Matter for Justice* (Illinois: University of Chicago Press, 2018), 7.

35. Darby and Rury, *The Color of Mind: Why the Origins of the Achievement Gap Matter for Justice*, 8.

36. Again, while *antiracist* is an option in our contemporary semantics, it clearly does not apply to the American education and economic systems.

37. For a good introduction to this topic, see Thomas Christiano, ed., *Philosophy and Democracy: An Anthology* (Oxford: Oxford University Press, 2003). We will not

be centering this question in the remainder of this book. See also Leland Harper, ed., *The Crisis of American Democracy: Essays on a Failing Institution* (Wilmington, DE: Vernon Press, 2022).

38. Any definition of democracy is sure to be contentious. We borrow this rough definition from Robert A. Dahl, *Democracy and its Critics* (New Haven: Yale University Press, 1991) and Thomas Christiano, *The Rule of the Many: Fundamental Issues in Democratic Theory* (Boulder, CO: Westview Press, 1996).

39. This is despite the fact that individual Black Americans sometimes do achieve positions of real power. Despite Mitch McConnell's insistence, individual success is not indicative of the end of group oppression.

40. Stacy Jones, "White Men Account for 72% of Corporate Leadership at 16 Fortune 500 Companies," *Fortune,* June 9, 2017.

41. Gillian B. White, "There are Currently 4 Black CEOs in the Fortune 500," *The Atlantic,* October 26, 2017.

42. Claire Hansen, "116th Congress by Party, Race, Gender, and Religion," *U.S. News & World Report,* January 3, 2019.

43. To put it bluntly, Blacks can't merit their way into the halls of social and political power because the substandard education with which they are provided doesn't enable that move, and they can't buy their way in because the knowledge gap precludes their acquisition of enough wealth to do so.

44. Darby and Rury, *The Color of Mind: Why the Origins of the Achievement Gap Matter for Justice,* 100–101.

45. Michelle Alexander, "The New Jim Crow," *Ohio State Journal of Criminal Law* 9, no. 1 (2011): 8.

46. Of course, Blacks still maintain the ability to indirectly influence who comes to occupy social and political positions of power. They can campaign, support the NAACP, the ACLU, or other similar political organizations, and engage in protest and civil disobedience, among other options. However, we maintain that the widespread permanent disenfranchisement of Black Americans via their mass incarceration, because it is a loss of direct influence, represents a fundamental loss of democratic power and control.

47. To provide yet another example of the phenomenon we identify, consider that one common response to Alexander from whites is that the people maintaining and upholding the criminal justice system are simply implementing the laws, and so cannot be racist. (And the laws themselves are surely not racist, because they make no explicit mention of race!) Our inability to describe the laws, and the people who uphold them, as unsettlingly race-based without falling into the false trinary of racist/not racist/antiracist thus blocks our ability to get the majority of whites to even see the problem, much less react appropriately to its existence and unjust effects.

48. See Megan Mitchell, "'White People, We Need to Stop being so Damn Fragile!': White and Male Fragility as Epistemic Arrogance," in *Pacifism, Politics, and Feminism: Intersections and Innovations,* ed. Jennifer Kling (Netherlands: Brill Rodopi, 2019), 51–67, for an approach of this sort.

49. One response here might be that it is not worth trying to fix the United States, because the racism is baked in, so to speak, to the system. We respond to this point below. Thanks to Colin Lewis for raising this point.

50. Among others, Bob Ditter, LCSW, child and family therapist, argues for this approach as the one most conducive to healthy child and adolescent development. Bob Ditter, *To Tell the Truth* (California: Healthy Learning, 2013). See also Sal Severe, *How to Behave so Your Children Will, Too!* (New York: Penguin Books, 2003).

51. The response here might well be that this unduly puts the burden back on the Black person, making it their responsibility to help the white person feel comfortable and come to understand their racism. Clearly, it is the responsibility of white people to come to understand, and work to change, their racist attitudes, actions, and unsettlingly race-based milieu. We are not here arguing that Black people are responsible for solving racial injustice; rather, we are arguing that it is worth adding some additional semantic tools to the antiracist toolbox, for those who feel able to use them. For more on this issue, see chapter six.

52. We discuss this question in depth in chapter four.

53. While the racist/not racist/antiracist semantic false trinary might have some positives, in that it is simple, clear, and easy to deploy linguistically, we maintain that the negatives we have outlined far outweigh these positives. Our point here is that the current semantic trinary, in addition to being false, is not clearly working to solve or even seriously ameliorate ongoing racial injustices and oppression in the United States. And in fact, assuming that our above analysis is correct, the opposite is true. So, some semantic expansion is needed.

54. See, among others, Peter French, ed., *Individual and Collective Responsibility* (Rochester, VT: Schenkman, 1998), 25; Joel Feinberg, "Collective Responsibility," *Journal of Philosophy* 65, no. 21 (1968): 687. We discuss this in depth in chapter four.

55. For more considerations related to the question of revolution, see Colin J. Lewis and Jennifer Kling, "Justified Revolution in Contemporary American Democracy: A Confucian-Inspired Account," in *The Crisis of American Democracy: Essays on a Failing Institution*, ed. Leland Harper (Wilmington, DE: Vernon Press, 2022), 167–92.

56. This might begin to sound like tone policing. However, we think that it is actually tone opening, in that we are advocating for the creation of more semantic terms and vocabulary, that will enable us to speak in many different tones, voices, and ways about race and race-based situations.

Chapter Three

COVID-19 in Black America

People who can sit on their couch at home please be responsible and do so. We can get through this together if we all do what's recommended.

—Hilary Duff[1]

At the time of writing, the world is still very much in the middle of a global pandemic: COVID-19.[2] While vaccines for COVID-19 have been developed and distributed, the availability and distribution of these vaccines, among other things, has been far from equitable. Particular groups in America (and more broadly) remain in high-risk situations, in terms of the medical, financial, and social consequences of the COVID-19 pandemic.

Racial undertones have been present in the discourse of COVID-19 since it was first declared a global pandemic by the World Health Organization (WHO) on March 11, 2020. Seen by many in the West, or at least in the United States, as a virus caused by "them" in the East that "we" now have to face, the otherism was deep-seated from the outset. Massive media coverage of the virus, frequently displaying stock photos of Asians while discussing the matter, and then–US president Donald Trump repeatedly referring to COVID-19 as "the Chinese virus," served only to perpetuate these views. Upticks in instances of violence against Asian people in major cities across the US further put on display the views held by a not-insignificant number of people: this shut down, these health concerns, this financial crisis, is *their* fault and *we* are paying for it. To be sure, the increased frequency and severity of racist thought and behavior against Asians is an essential and worthy topic for discussion, especially as it relates both to institutional and personal responses to being faced with a global pandemic. For our purposes here, however, our focus will remain largely on the status of Black America and the position in which it finds itself in the age of COVID-19.

Becoming more prominent in discussions of this pandemic is the negative impact that the actions (or inactions) of the US federal government continue to have on Black America. The consequences faced by the Black community because of the United States' inability to manage this crisis properly are unique when compared to those faced by white Americans, and this puts members of the Black community at far greater risk not only to contract the virus and suffer the associated symptoms up to and including death, but also to suffer long-term and generational setbacks in their efforts to improve their socioeconomic status. To put it plainly, Black Americans are more susceptible to deeper, generational, defining losses than are white Americans, but the semantic false trinary precludes fruitful conversations about this aspect of the dynamic disaster of racism and potential solutions. We are prevented from moving forward since we cannot properly describe the institutional and interpersonal nature of some of these problems.

Our goal in this chapter is to highlight the *unique* challenges that have been, are currently being, and will be faced by Black Americans regarding COVID-19 and to punctuate that these difficulties reflect, and are exacerbated by, the United States' historical and ongoing dynamic disaster of institutionalized racism and racial oppression. This discussion is presented in very general terms; there is no doubt that some, or perhaps even many, Black Americans are in far better positions than many white Americans with respect to the medical and socioeconomic consequences of COVID-19. However, we approach these topics from a macro perspective rather than focusing on particular, individual circumstances. This approach better takes account of the fluid nature of the data with which we are working. It also dispels as inappropriate any potential responses that run parallel to the "racism is dead because we had a Black president" line of thought.[3]

It is vital to keep in mind that, at the time of writing this chapter, we are still very much in the middle of the pandemic. Much of the world's economy is still shut down, many international borders are closed, and the science is still unclear on the symptoms, transmissibility, and possible treatments for COVID-19. As such, the data used to supply the arguments in this chapter may very well change in the coming months and years. New data emerging over time may serve either to invalidate or to further support the arguments made, though it is far more likely that emerging data will serve only to further support our position.

In the following sections, we detail several factors regarding the COVID-19 situation that are unique to Black Americans and so legitimately contribute to an increased level of concern, regarded both in qualitative terms (how deep the type of concern is) and quantitative terms (how many concerns are present). Ultimately, each of the considerations discussed below, individually, is enough to provoke legitimate concern in any sensible person—but Black Americans, by and large, must face, will face, or are facing the cumulative consequences of all of these considerations. Be it individually or cumulatively, these threats with which Black Americans are faced put them in a unique and undesirable position. Black Americans, in the age of COVID-19, disproportionately face natural and human-made threats of destroyed ideals, rapidly deteriorating health conditions, death, generational poverty, destruction of familial and social networks, and loss of dignity. As Black American philosopher and St. Louis University professor Yolonda Wilson writes,

> The intimate familiarity with death in this pandemic becomes one of the ways it is clear to me that I occupy two worlds—one overwhelmingly white, well-resourced, and for whom pandemic deaths are largely an abstraction, while the other is decidedly Black and intimately and repeatedly touched by sickness and death. . . .

My friend and sometime research partner, Akilah Jefferson Shah (a brilliant allergy immunologist who trained at NIH under Dr. Fauci himself), wrote an article for the *Huffington Post* last summer about the devastating impact of the COVID-19 pandemic on Black communities. She writes,

> *During a recent Zoom conference call with colleagues, I suddenly realized that, while I have had several family members, friends, and acquaintances who have fallen ill with and died of COVID-19, my colleagues have had none. The single obvious difference between my colleagues and me? I am Black, and New Orleans is my hometown.*

My hometown, Albany, Georgia, was also a hotspot early in the pandemic—at its worst, it followed only Wuhan, China, and Lombardy, Italy, in cases per capita. Indeed, at the very moment that New York was dominating the news as the pandemic "epicenter" in the United States, my small south Georgia town of 75,000 was a global hotspot, with more cases per capita than New York City. Every day I watched helplessly from Durham, NC (where my fellowship at the National Humanities Center was being interrupted), and later from Washington, DC (where I returned home rather than sit alone in my one bedroom apartment in Durham), and I wondered if that would be the day that I would lose my mother, if I would become an orphan, become unmoored—having lost my father years earlier and my twin sister at birth. I wondered how it would feel the first time I returned to Albany and passed by houses that were now empty, as Covid wiped entire households off the map. How would it feel to attend church with my mother for the first time and see empty spaces where people who shaped me during my formative years once occupied seats in pews?

Members of my family fell ill, and I am grateful that none died. However, I am deeply traumatized. Still. Despite the excitement of a new job in St. Louis, I write and work through molasses. It seems as though every third email I send these days begins, "Thank you for your patience . . ." or "Please forgive my delayed response . . ." It feels impossible to explain the depths of this trauma to those who occupy this other world, those for whom 18 straight months of intimate connection to illness, death, and loss is largely an abstraction. At the same time, I'm not sure what would be different if I *could* explain. I hear so much talk about being "back to normal." Meanwhile, I struggle to figure out what "normal" is.[4]

THE JUSTICE SYSTEM AND COVID-19

As early as March 2020, it was becoming clear that prison populations were among the hardest hit by COVID-19 in the United States. All major news outlets agreed, regardless of political leanings: COVID-19 spread rapidly among inmates.[5] The conditions in many US correctional facilities left them in no position to manage a healthcare crisis such as this properly. Of the conditions at one prison, it was noted that "Inmates have no access to gloves or proper masks and have only cold water to wash their hands."[6] Failing to provide inmates with proper personal protective equipment while still requiring them to cohabitate with one another in such close quarters meant that these inmates could not follow the most basic precautions for personal protection set out by the WHO. This is precisely the kind of situation that allowed, and continues to allow, the rapid spread of a highly infectious virus among a specific population. These inmates have no way of protecting themselves and nowhere to go to escape possible infection. They are purely at the mercy of the virus. And in the likely[7] event that they contract COVID-19, the quantity and quality of individualized medical care that these inmates receive is severely limited. This has become such a pressing matter that multiple federal lawsuits have been launched, seeking the release of many prisoners with underlying medical conditions for fear of their health if they were to remain in custody.[8] The US prison system is quite simply unable to provide any level of assurance for the safety of the inmates for whom it is tasked with caring. This is not to discount the good work being done by individuals within that system—it is rather to point toward an institutional issue: the prison system is such that it cannot protect inmates from COVID-19 (or, for that matter, any extremely infectious disease).[9]

The US prison population is in a devastatingly unique position in terms of COVID-19 contractability, transmissibility, and treatment. As we explained in chapter two, Michelle Alexander famously argues that mass incarceration in the United States is a continuing assault on Black America.[10] "The United States has more people behind bars than any other nation, a total incarcerated population of nearly 2.3 million as of 2017, including nearly 1.5 million in state and federal prisons and another 745,000 in local jails."[11] Of the total number of individuals who are incarcerated, depending on the data source, the percentage of inmates who are Black ranges between 35 percent and 40 percent. Blacks are drastically over-represented in the United States correctional system. This invites further discussion, which we began in chapter two. For our purposes here, though, we focus on the simple fact that in the country that incarcerates the highest number of people in the world, Blacks are shockingly over-represented. Combine this over-representation with the COVID-19 contractability, transmissibility, and treatment problems endemic in the prison system. Conclusion: this is a problem that has disproportionately negative direct consequences for the Black community.

One possible response to all of this is that the failure of the United States government to provide adequate protection from and treatment for COVID-19 within the prison system is, on the surface, not a race issue—it is a class issue. The class of people who are suffering the consequences from this inability to manage the pandemic properly is the class of people who have been convicted of crimes and who are currently serving sentences (plus the prison staff, who have nominally chosen to be there). But this kind of response overlooks the fact that the population in question is predominantly Black. Just as one could say that the 2016 mass shooting that killed fifty at Pulse Nightclub in Orlando, Florida, was an assault on nightclub-goers, this overlooks the meaningful detail that the majority of those killed inside the club that night were members of the LGBTQ+ community. And, just as it would be irresponsible to overlook that element with the Pulse Nightclub tragedy, which was clearly an assault on the LGBTQ+ community, it is similarly irresponsible to overlook the current situation in the US prison system and its response to COVID-19, which is clearly an assault on the Black community.[12]

PUNITIVE DISENFRANCHISEMENT

A secondary concern, closely related to the concerning number of Black Americans who are incarcerated and the conditions of the correctional facilities during this pandemic, is that many members of the Black community have been stripped of their right to vote as the result of felony disenfranchisement. Extending far beyond prison walls, many Black Americans continue to be limited in various ways as a result of felony convictions long after serving their last day in prison. This is something on which Michelle Alexander

Table 3.1.   Disenfranchisement by State—Estimated disenfranchisement rates for African Americans and non-African Americans in select US States.[1]

	Non-African American Disenfranchisement Rate	African American Disenfranchisement Rate
Arizona	3.88%	11.2%
Nevada	3.46%	12.6%
Mississippi	5.22%	13.92%
Alabama	4.57%	14.98%
Wyoming	5.86%	18.29%
Tennessee	4.80%	18.92%
Virginia	4.21%	20.37%
Kentucky	6.11%	22.34%
Florida	8.13%	23.32%

1. Uggen, Shannon and Manza, *State-Level Estimates of Felon Disenfranchisement in the United States, 2010*, 17–18.

focuses much of her attention (as noted in chapter two). The inability to vote in the years leading up to this pandemic has meant that, since it is the legislators and public officials who are guiding us through this pandemic, the Black community is at the mercy of those whom they had no voice in electing or appointing. Again, Black Americans are in the position of being subject to authoritarian rule rather than being (possibly) active participants in democratic rule. As recently as late 2016, it was estimated that the total number of votes lost to felony disenfranchisement was 6.1 million.[13] Data from 2010, furthermore, tells us that Black Americans nationally lose their civil rights, including voting rights, at four times the rate of non-Black Americans.[14] (See Table 3.1 for some state-by-state data.) This is not surprising, given the overrepresentation of Blacks under the control of the US prison system.[15]

A disproportionate number of Blacks are at risk in sub-standard conditions in America's jails and prisons and, for years leading up to now, have not had the opportunity to directly impact the political processes that are now guiding pandemic response. Furthermore, as Blacks have had their political voices substantially silenced, when facing a healthcare crisis, the unique concerns of Black America are not heard through official channels,[16] and they are left with little to no recourse or say in the institutional pandemic response. This is yet another example of the Black community having to take a back seat and play the cards that their oppressors have dealt them.

To be clear, we don't know what the world would be like if Black Americans were democratically included in the pandemic response. It could be equally bad, worse, or better. The point though, is that the Black community has been disproportionately precluded from participating in the democratic process and this silencing of Black voices has prevented Blacks from having any direct say over some of the most fundamental aspects of their lives such as health, safety, and finances. Though this is not necessarily a new phenomenon (in fact it is a very old phenomenon), COVID-19 serves to illuminate the injustice that has been, and continues to be, faced by a significant segment of the American population.

You might think that although Black Americans are precluded from direct democratic impact and control, they still have the opportunity to impact pandemic response and other institutional actions indirectly, via the American tradition of protest. In tandem with COVID-19 are the global #BlackLivesMatter (BLM) protests that took shape following the murder of George Floyd by Minneapolis police officer Derek Chauvin. The protests call for, among other things, an end to police brutality which, in far too many cases, ends in the death of unarmed Black men. These peaceful protests (of the over 7,500 BLM demonstrations that occurred in the United States in 2020, 95 percent of them were nonviolent)[17] went on for several months and garnered international media coverage.

In response, legislative changes were introduced that highlight the dynamic disaster that is American antiBlack racism. In late August 2020, the then–governor of Tennessee, Bill Lee, signed a bill putting in place harsher penalties for protestors. The Associated Press writes that "[m]ost notably, the new law now states that those who illegally camp on state property would now face a Class E felony, punishable by up to six years in prison, rather than a misdemeanor. Felony convictions in Tennessee result in the revocation of an individual's right to vote."[18] Camping on state property has been a tactic commonly employed by BLM protesters—they often camp on the lawns of the state's Capitol building to demand legislative action. It is painfully ironic that, in demanding legislative changes to combat institutional racism through nonviolent protest, one of the only meaningful legislative changes that the predominantly Black movement has brought about (at least in Tennessee) is a law that exacerbates the very same systemic racism that is being protested. Furthermore, this law precludes any protesters who are convicted of violating it from trying to bring about meaningful change in precisely the way that we assume the legislators would like: voting. In essence, what is being told to Black Americans is that their fundamental rights can, and will, be revoked as a punishment for exercising their fundamental rights. This leaves them increasingly subject to authoritarian control and exacerbates the injustice at issue.

None of the considerations discussed above even touch on the subject of disenfranchisement through other, non-punitive, avenues. By this, we mean instances where individuals are legally entitled to vote but cannot *actually* vote because of any number of socioeconomic considerations. We have previously addressed this issue in chapter two, noting that whereas many

Black Americans can vote, they really can't. By this, we mean that Blacks are overrepresented in blue-collar, hourly jobs that "do not tend to afford workers the time they would need to even potentially exercise their supposed rights, as citizens living in a purportedly democratic system, to various kinds of standard political engagement."[19] These jobs do not offer their employees the opportunity to exercise their right to vote in part because of shift work that takes place during polling hours. Further, even if workers in these jobs *could* get the time off, there is no guarantee that they are in the position to take this time, given the likely potential that they cannot afford to miss out on the pay that they would have earned had they kept working during that time. Additionally, the financial implications relating to transportation, childcare, and personal health and mobility, to name a few, all work together to preclude Black Americans from exercising their supposed right to vote. (For the philosophers playing along at home, this is the distinction between *de dicto* and *de facto* rights.) This leaves Black Americans with little to no voice in the legislative processes that govern their lives and, in this particular case, their physical health, safety, and well-being as it pertains to COVID-19. The complexities of these systems and the individuals who uphold them through their everyday actions, however, cannot be comprehensively discussed currently without invoking the semantic false trinary of racist/not racist/antiracist, which triggers white fragility, which in turn blocks any forward progress.

UNDERLYING HEALTH CONDITIONS

One of the primary predictors for who is more likely to suffer severe complications if infected with COVID-19 is the presence of existing underlying health conditions. Those individuals who have a history of pre-existing health conditions are more likely to require hospitalization, are more likely to be admitted to the intensive care unit, and are more likely to die if they contract COVID-19.[20] Black Americans suffer from pre-existing health conditions at a far higher rate than do white Americans. The reasons for this can be debated, with some arguing that the root cause is genetic, others arguing that it is socioeconomic. In contrast, others argue that it is merely a matter of lifestyle choice.[21] Regardless of the cause,[22] the overall health of Black Americans before the COVID-19 pandemic was far worse than the overall health of white Americans. Blacks, even when age, income, and education are controlled for, have been and continue to be significantly more prone to suffer from, among other things, high blood pressure, diabetes, and stroke.[23] These factors lead to disproportionately high rates of Blacks dying at younger ages when all causes are considered. This is especially true in cases of preventable or treatable illnesses.[24] The fact of the matter is that Blacks are more suscep-tible and more likely to suffer from serious health complications if and when infected with COVID-19. This in itself, puts Blacks in a unique and unfavor-able position. Although whites don't like to or are unable to acknowledge it because of their fragility, Black America started off facing this pandemic, from a health perspective, in the red.

THE WEALTH GAP

Black America possesses significantly less wealth than white America, both as a whole and per capita. This space will not be used to provide a series of statistics, as this fact is (or should be) common knowledge. It is old news that the average white American family has a net worth nearly ten times that of the average Black American family. The numbers associated with these percent-ages amount to $171,000 and $17,150, respectively.[25] These numbers mean that "[o]ne out of three Black children grows up in poverty while only one out of ten white children lives in poverty."[26] Black America is already operating, financially, on a razor's edge, with almost no cushion to help soften the blow from even the slightest economic bump, let alone from a historic economic crash. This wealth gap should be stunning; however, people's widespread apathy in response indicates that they are not seeing it for the disaster that it is.

Eddie S. Glaude Jr. discusses the bleak financial situation of Black America in his 2017 book *Democracy in Black: How Race Still Enslaves the American Soul*. In *Democracy in Black*, Glaude Jr.'s discussion of Black wealth (or lack thereof) comes in the context of the 2008 recession, which brought about what he calls "The Great Black Depression."[27] However, many of the consid-erations and consequences that he discusses are still relevant today. Glaude Jr. acknowledges that there was widespread financial devastation for people of all backgrounds across America and that the road to recovery would be a multi-year effort for many people. A bleak outlook, to be sure. "But in Black America, the reality was even bleaker," writes Glaude Jr.[28] He continues, "I mean this beyond the familiar platitude that says 'whenever white America has a cold, Black America has the flu.' The reality is that by every relevant statistical measure (employment, wages, wealth, etc.) Black America has experienced and is experiencing a depression. This is more like the symptoms of a national congenital disease than the flu."[29]

While written about an altogether different crisis, the words of Glaude Jr. seem eerily, almost frighteningly, applicable to the current situation. Even down to the symbolic use of "cold" and "flu." Black America is simply far closer to hitting rock bottom, financially, than is white America. With the widespread disruption of global economic markets brought on by COVID-19, many people have seen or will see their wealth substantially decrease. This is not a significant problem for those who have a higher net worth and who have "rainy day reserves" to help mitigate the disruption of their everyday lives by decreased or suspended income. But, by and large, Black Americans do not fit into that category. Many, if not most, Black Americans are still recovering from The Great Black Depression of 2008.

As a result of the 2008 recession, "African Americans lost 31 percent of their wealth between 2007 and 2010. White Americans lost 11 percent. By 2009, 35 percent of African American households had zero or negative net worth. According to the Pew Research Center, by 2011, Black families had lost 53 percent of their wealth."[30] These figures are staggering, both in terms of the sheer wealth lost and in the comparative discrepancies of the wealth lost between Black American families and white American families. Recovering from this and building up any meaningful wealth for Black Americans was and still is, in many cases, extremely difficult. This is especially the case when we consider the unemployment figures that typically accompany an economic crisis. Unemployment numbers soared in 2008. We have seen them soar even higher in 2020—but again, the burden of unemployment, just like the privilege of wealth, is not shared proportionally. In a discussion of 2008, Glaude Jr. writes, "[o]ften the last hired and the first fired, people saw Black unemployment soar as a result of the economic collapse. So much so that by November 2010, national Black unemployment reached the stunning level of 16 percent (and this figure does not include those who simply dropped out of the labor market). White unemployment stood at 9 percent."[31] Glaude Jr. continues, "in short, the terrible effects of the Great Black Depression guarantee, unless we fully understand the urgency of now, that even darker days are ahead . . . [b]ut what's really scary is how little anyone outside [B]lack America seems to care."[32] It is absolutely clear that Glaude Jr. was correct in his assessment that darker days would be ahead since, at the time of writing, we are in them.

By all indicators, the economic crisis brought on by COVID-19 is the worst of its kind in a generation. When combined with the already-precarious position of Black American wealth, it is likely that this pandemic will result in Blacks being overrepresented among those who suffer catastrophic financial losses, to the point that it will take generations to rebuild. To be sure, this will be the case for many white Americans as well but, as discussed above, Black Americans face further impediments to achieving financial security that white Americans do not.

By holding less wealth, not only does it mean that Black America is far closer to the brink of financial ruin as a result of the downturn in global markets than is white America, but it also means that Black Americans are significantly handicapped with regard to the measures that they can take to prevent themselves from contracting, transmitting, and suffering from the more severe symptoms of the virus and disease. Many of the recommendations from the WHO, the Centers for Disease Control and Prevention (CDC) in the United States, and local community health organizations around the world amounted to "stay home from work," "spend more time in open, well-ventilated, outdoor areas," "avoid frequent trips to the store," and "avoid close contact with anybody and everybody." All of these recommendations would help to flatten the curve of infection rates; however, the simple fact of the matter is they are not feasible for many Black American families. Each of these recommendations, much like the epigraph to this chapter (which was echoed by other celebrities and public figures worldwide) presupposes a certain socioeconomic position. The reality is that many, if not most, Black Americans are not in such a position; thus, they cannot follow any or all of these prescriptions.

Because of the relative lack of wealth of most Black American families, staying home from work for any prolonged period is not viable. Just as it may not be an available option for Black employees to take a day off work to vote, that same employee is likely not in a financial position to stay home from work so as to avoid potential exposure to COVID-19. As such, many Black Americans are put in the position of having to decide between staying home from work and missing out on income that would likely go toward essential things such as food, medication, rent or utilities, or going to work and facing potential exposure to the virus. It is also worth noting that, in the latter of these two options, with the increased chances of virus exposure comes the increased chances of virus infection, which would then result in the inability to work for approximately two weeks (depending both on local, state, and federal regulations and the severity of symptoms). In either case, Black Americans having to choose between physical health and financial well-being become more susceptible to other financial pitfalls, such as predatory lending. Being in this position has forced many Black employees to opt to go to work and face the potential danger of the virus rather than the definite danger of not earning sufficient money. This level of structural coercion amounts to injustice.

The relative lack of wealth held by Black America also prevents many Black families from being able to spend time in open, well-ventilated, outdoor areas. Many Black Americans live in urban city centers where large, open, outdoor areas are not often available or easily accessible. Not to mention when they do enjoy public parks and other outdoor spaces, they are at increased risk of having the police called on them unnecessarily by white people, especially white women (often pejoratively called "Karens").[33] Not living in the suburbs or rural areas, where green space is more prevalent, Blacks are likely to spend more time inside or in densely populated outdoor spaces. This makes the ability to physically distance from others much more difficult than it may otherwise be for those who live in less densely populated areas, such as the suburbs or rural areas. Finally, the homes that Blacks occupy in urban areas are often either smaller or house more people. Because of these smaller and fuller homes, storage space is more likely to be at a premium, making it more challenging to stockpile essential goods (if they even have the financial resources to purchase the extra goods in the first place). Lacking the financial ability to buy essential items in bulk, and lacking the requisite space to store these items properly, means that Black Americans are more likely to have to visit the store more frequently than white Americans which, again, puts them at a higher risk of a) coming into contact with the virus, b) contracting the virus, and c) being hospitalized (due to the likelihood of more severe symptoms, which is partially a function of underlying health conditions).

Given all of these considerations, which are directly and indirectly tied to wealth, it is the case that Black Americans are often, at best, faced with the difficult decision between adhering to the advice provided by the WHO, the CDC, and local community health organizations, and earning enough money to support their essential needs. At worst, that decision is made for them by their particular circumstances. This is a lose-lose situation for Black America, and one that is institutional rather than individual or interpersonal.

Black Americans face many additional problems that white Americans do not, in nearly every facet of their lives. This is no surprise, as academics have, for years, created terms to denote the various discrepancies between Black and white America, like the knowledge gap, the wealth gap, the achievement gap, the value gap, the military gap, and so forth (see chapter two for more on these gaps). But now we are in a global pandemic. The COVID-19 pandemic not only illuminates all of those gaps, but also widens them (or has the potential to widen them) significantly.

WHY DOES ANY OF THIS MATTER?

A simple question that can be asked, at this point, is "Why does any of this matter?" since many of the claims presented in this chapter seem evident to anybody who is *really* seeing what is going on. The pandemic as experienced by Black America is wholly different than the pandemic as experienced by white America. Although this "obvious fact" is simply overlooked by many, its result is that the moral and epistemic judgments many white Americans make about Black Americans' pandemic responses are at best, ill-informed, and, at worst, pernicious. They fail to recognize or understand the particular risks that are involved due to racial identity. It is as if they assume that the considerations are the same for everybody when that is simply not the case. Some people, or groups, have far more to lose than others. The socioeconomic, sociopolitical, and sociohistorical differences between Black and white America, and the ways in which those differences contour and constrain possible responses to the COVID-19 pandemic, are not apparent to all, and this is an opportunity to make them clear.

This discussion of the unique positioning of Black Americans in relation to the COVID-19 pandemic is essential and relevant because of the role that perception and experience plays in influencing our interpersonal and institutional behavior. Understanding different individual and group circumstances is likely to contribute to nuanced discussions about whether we should re-open restaurants, resume face-to-face instruction in schools, mandate vaccines and boosters, provide relief of various kinds, and judge people for their interpersonal practices of social distancing and mask-wearing. How we ought to go about situating our lives, actions, and institutions regarding the COVID-19 pandemic depends on integrating these differential considerations, rather than disregarding them.

One of the central problems that remains, however, and which exacerbates some of the issues discussed above, is our current inability to accurately describe and discuss these exact issues. For example, vaccine hesitancy in the Black American community is just one of the many complex discussions around COVID-19 that needs to be considered with sensitivity and depth at both the interpersonal and institutional levels, but currently can't be because we lack the appropriate semantic resources to do so. Such conversations are verboten because they can only take place via an invocation of the semantic false trinary, which in turn triggers white fragility. This immediately stops the conversation before any meaningful discussion can take place. It is unlikely that we can, at least in regular conversation, say that the COVID-19 pandemic or the United States' institutional, and Americans' interpersonal, response to it is *racist*, *not racist*, or *antiracist*. Those terms simply do not fit. As such, we need a proper term (or multiple terms) that accurately describes the racial intricacies of the COVID-19 pandemic in which we currently find ourselves, the responses to the pandemic, and the agents who are responsible for those responses. The lack of semantic expansion results in people's inability, and in some cases, their unwillingness, to engage in fruitful dialogue on this incredibly pressing issue. This results in the maintenance of the status quo—Black America remains subject to injustice and oppression.

NOTES

1. "What Smokey Robinson, Matthew McConaughey and More Stars are Saying about COVID-19." *USA Today,* updated November 26, 2021.

2. This chapter was originally published by Leland Harper as "Fear and the Importance of Race-Based Data in COVID-19 Policy Implementation," *Global Discourse: An Interdisciplinary Journal of Current Affairs* 11, no. 3 (2021): 433–39. Our thanks to the journal for granting us permission to republish it here with alterations. A more accessible version of the ideas presented in the article is published online at https://www.transformingsociety.co.uk/2021/05/19/black-america-and-fear-race -based-data-as-a-tool-for-effective-covid-19-policy/.

3. This also brings to mind when Mitch McConnell said, to paraphrase, that paying reparations for slavery was a bad idea because a Black president had already been elected. His comments on reparations are, in some respects, the inspiration for writing this book. See the Preface for more on this issue.

4. Yolonda Wilson, "A Time for Grief, Not 'Resilience,'" *Daily Nous,* November 22, 2021.

5. "Coronavirus in the U.S.: Latest Map and Case Count." *New York Times,* updated May 3, 2020; Hollie Silverman, "Coronavirus is Tearing through Prison and Jail Populations in Ohio and Illinois," *CNN,* April 20, 2020; Danielle Wallace, "Chicago Jail Becomes Top Coronavirus Hot Spot, Exceeding Cases Aboard USS *Roosevelt*," *Fox News,* April 9, 2020; C. J. Ciaramella, "8 of the Top 10 Biggest U.S. Coronavirus Hotspots are Prisons and Jails," *Reason,* April 29, 2020; Ned Parker et al., "Spread of Coronavirus Accelerates in U.S. Jails and Prisons," *Reuters,* March 28, 2020.

6. Parker et al., "Spread of Coronavirus Accelerates in U.S. Jails and Prisons."

7. We use "likely" in the relative sense. It may not be likely that all inmates at correctional facilities are likely to be infected with COVID-19, but the data does seem to suggest that those in the prison population are *more* likely to contract the virus than those who are not.

8. Timothy Williams and Danielle Ivory, "Chicago's Jail is Top U.S. Hot Spot as Virus Spreads Behind Bars," *New York Times,* April 8, 2020.

9. Before smallpox was eradicated, it used to sweep through correctional facilities. Deborah Oxley, "'The Seat of Death and Terror': Urbanization, Stunting, and Smallpox," *The Economic History Review* 56, no. 4 (2003): 623–56.

10. Michelle Alexander, *The New Jim Crow: Mass Incarceration in the Age of Colorblindness* (New York: The New Press, 2012).

11. Parker et al., "Spread of Coronavirus Accelerates in U.S. Jails and Prisons."

12. This may not be the perfect analogy, as there are notable differences between the two situations. The first is that the clubgoers in the Pulse incident were, presumably, there voluntarily and free to come and go as they pleased while the same cannot be said of prisoners. The second is that the gunman in the Pulse incident seemed to have a clear intent to harm members of the LGBTQ+ community, while it cannot so easily be said that the US government has a clear intent to harm members of the Black community. (We do think only a small step is needed to reach this conclusion,

though.) The analogy holds, however, in the sense that looking at each incident in the broadest terms skews the reality of the situation: that one particular minoritized group is being harmed more than others.

13. Christopher Uggen, Ryan Larson and Sarah Shannon, "6 Million Lost Voters: State-Level Estimates of Felony Disenfranchisement, 2016," *The Sentencing Project,* October 6, 2016.

14. Christopher Uggen, Sarah Shannon and Jeff Manza, *State-Level Estimates of Felon Disenfranchisement in the United States, 2010* (The Sentencing Project: Washington, D.C., 2012), 12.

15. Steven Swartzer, "Punishment and Democratic Rights: A Case Study in Non-Ideal Penal Theory," in *The Ethics of Policing and Imprisonment,* eds. Molly Gardner and Michael Weber (New York: Palgrave Macmillan, 2018), 7–37.

16. Or at least not heard in any way that demands urgent and meaningful institutional response.

17. ACLED, *A Year of Racial Justice Protests: Key Trends in Demonstrations Supporting the BLM Movement,* The Armed Conflict Location & Event Data Project, acleddata.com, 2021.

18. Kimberlee Kruesi and Jonathan Mattise, "Tennessee Gov Signs Bill Upping Penalties on some Protests," *AP News,* August 21, 2020.

19. Jennifer Kling and Leland Harper, "The Semantic Foundations of White Fragility and the Consequences for Justice," *Res Philosophica* 97, no. 2 (2020), 338. doi:10.11612/resphil.1891.

20. Jan Kobal (dir.), "This Pandemic," *Coronavirus, Explained,* Netflix, 2020.

21. David McBride provides a concise historical account of the Black experience in American healthcare, covering from the civil war through to Hurricane Katrina. David McBride, *Caring for Equality: A History of African American Health and Healthcare* (Lanham, MD: Rowman & Littlefield, 2018).

22. The reason we do not engage with debates about the various causes of pre-existing health conditions is because the import of such debates does not matter for the ethical treatment of patients. Medical professionals, as well as bioethicists, conclude that it is generally impermissible to allow such factors to impact how or whether patients are treated. Medical professionals don't refuse to treat the lung cancer of a lifelong smoker, or the car crash victim who was speeding.

23. "African American Health: Creating Equal Opportunities for Health." *Centers for Disease Control and Prevention,* July 3, 2017.

24. "African American Health: Creating Equal Opportunities for Health."

25. Kriston McIntosh et al., "Examining the Black-White Wealth Gap," *Brookings,* February 27, 2020.

26. Eddie S. Glaude Jr., *Democracy in Black: How Race Still Enslaves the American Soul* (New York: Broadway Books, 2017), 19.

27. Glaude Jr., *Democracy in Black: How Race Still Enslaves the American Soul,* 17.

28. Glaude Jr., *Democracy in Black: How Race Still Enslaves the American Soul,* 18.

29. Glaude Jr., *Democracy in Black: How Race Still Enslaves the American Soul,*
18.

30. Glaude Jr., *Democracy in Black: How Race Still Enslaves the American Soul,*
18.

31. Glaude Jr., *Democracy in Black: How Race Still Enslaves the American Soul,*
19.

32. Glaude Jr., *Democracy in Black: How Race Still Enslaves the American Soul,*
20.

33. For example, Amy Cooper, a white dog owner, called the police on Black bird-watcher Christian Cooper after he asked her to leash her dog in New York's Central Park. David K. Li, "Charge Dropped Against White Woman Who Called Police on Black Bird-Watcher," *NBC News,* February 16, 2021. For numerous examples of this kind of race-based behavior, see Bill Hutchinson, "From 'BBQ Becky' to 'Golfcart Gail,' List of Unnecessary 911 Calls made on Blacks Continues to Grow," *ABC News,* October 19, 2018. This list includes the infamous BBQ Becky, Golfcart Gail, and Cornerstone Caroline.

Chapter Four

Shifting Toward Democracy and Justice

What we speak becomes the house we live in.

—Sufi poet Hafiz[1]

In previous chapters, we argued that the semantics of racism fall squarely into the political realm, as well as the ethical realm, because the semantic false trinary of racist/not racist/antiracist partially undergirds and perpetuates the existence of the dynamic disaster of racism, which in turn supports two political systems in the United States: democracy for whites, and authoritarianism for Blacks. In this chapter, we first borrow from W. E. B. Du Bois's understanding of democracy to deepen and extend this argument, contending that democracy for all requires an expanded semantics of the sort we describe. The political institution of democracy demands community; and to build community in the United States, given its history and ongoing racism, we need new and better ways of talking to each other about racial oppression and injustice.

However, we are sensitive to the concern, prominently expressed in Charles Mills's *The Racial Contract*, that liberal democracy has white supremacy woven through it.[2] Although Mills himself doesn't do so, this worry has led many to reject democracy as an ideal. So, we turn in the latter half of the chapter to Iris Marion Young's model of justice, which is concerned not with democracy specifically, but rather with moving societies away from injustice and oppression more broadly. Following Young, we have an obligation to work toward justice in a variety of ways, because we are responsible—in the sense of being accountable—for the presence of injustice in our societies. One way of moving toward justice is to create the expanded semantics we describe, in order to generate the sorts of conversations that are likely to lead to more just practices and social structures. Ultimately, if you care about the attainment of democracy for all, or more broadly about justice more equally enjoyed by all (and you should!), an expanded semantics of racism is a necessary stepping stone to these goals.

BUILDING A DU BOISIAN DEMOCRACY

In chapter two, we introduced a standard understanding of democracy in Western analytic philosophy. Democracy is a method of collective decision making wherein the participants have a rough kind of equality in the decision-making process, and so can be said to have roughly equal impact on, or control over, that process and its results.[3] For instance, a person might say that the United States is a democracy because each person has one vote (rough equality in the decision-making process), and so each person has an equal impact on the results (no one person has full control, but together, all American voters have collective control over who gets elected). Now, this is not how the American political system actually operates; but if the members of the United States wanted to have a fully democratic system, they could work to make this description accurate.

Black Americans do not live in a democracy, on this standard conceptual understanding of democracy, because they do not have the kind of equality required (as compared to white Americans). As we argued in chapters two and three, they do not have roughly equal impact on, or control over, the formal political decision-making processes of the United States, because of the dynamic disaster of racism. Mass incarceration, in conjunction with the knowledge gap and wealth gap, as well as the straightforward voter suppression that has occurred since the 2013 gutting, by the US Supreme Court, of the Voting Rights Act of 1965,[4] all combine to make it the case that Black Americans do not enjoy even minimal formal democratic equality, much less the robust civic equality and agency called for in W. E. B. Du Bois's conception of democracy.

Du Bois argues that democracy, properly understood, requires more than simply rough equality within the formal mechanisms of the state's collective decision-making processes.[5] Democracy, rather, is community-oriented and conversation-based. Co-members in the political project must build together the types of systems and practices that they want to exist, that recognize each person in the community as a member of that community who has worth and standing, and whose dignity ought to be respected by the political processes of which they are a part. For example, think about deciding which restaurant to go to with your group of best friends. You wouldn't have a blind vote—you'd talk about it, weigh people's preferences, feelings, and needs, and try to make a decision that is genuinely good for everyone. Democratic justice is not about formal sameness, according to Du Bois, but rather about the right to be recognized as a person who is a member of the community with input to provide, regardless of their peculiarities. He writes:

> The equality in political, industrial, and social life which modern men must have in order to live, is not to be confounded with sameness. On the contrary, in our case, it is rather insistence upon the right of diversity;—upon the right of a human being to be a man even if he does not wear the same cut of vest, the same curl of hair or the same color of skin. Human equality does not even entail, as it is sometimes said, absolute equality of opportunity; for certainly the natural inequalities of inherent genius and varying gift make this a dubious phrase. But there is a more and more clearly recognized minimum of opportunity and maximum of freedom to be, to move and to think, which the modern world denies to no being which it recognizes as a real man.[6]

It is in part this recognition of the right of diversity within a community that leads to civic equality and democratic agency. To be clear, Du Bois regards the fight for the vote as essential—he argues that Black Americans must fight for their right to engage in the formal political mechanisms available to them as citizens of the US. However, the franchise is not sufficient for democratic justice, because voting is compatible with civic inequality—you can vote and still lack the freedom to think and converse openly about difficult issues (racial and otherwise) within society.[7] Also necessary for democracy is the creation of a political community that seeks out and values input from all of its members, and that has the capacity to respond productively to such critical conversations. As Du Bois puts it, "Honest and earnest criticism from those whose interests are most nearly touched—criticism of writers by readers, of government by those governed, of leaders by those led—this is the soul of democracy and the safeguard of modern society."[8] To call back to our discussion of COVID-19 in the previous chapter, it is not enough to simply note the existence of the wealth gap and vote for politicians who promise to solve it; what needs to happen is that whites need to take into account the ways in which the pandemic uniquely and differentially affects Black America, which they cannot do without listening to Black Americans and incorporating their concerns into interpersonal and institutional responses.

In his analysis of the American South, Du Bois argues that there is no recognition of the right of diversity within that community, and so no space for the kind of honest criticism which is essential to democracy. As he writes, Black Americans in the South, in their own defense, must engage in deception and silence, which on the one hand keeps them alive, but on the other hand fosters oppression and tyranny. He says:

> Today the young Negro of the South who would succeed cannot be frank and outspoken, honest and self-assertive, but rather he is daily tempted to be silent and wary, politic and sly; he must flatter and be pleasant, endure petty insults with a smile, shut his eyes to wrong; in too many cases he sees positive personal advantage in deception and lying. His real thoughts, his real aspirations, must be guarded in whispers; he must not criticise, he must not complain. Patience, humility, and adroitness must, in these growing [B]lack youth, replace impulse, manliness, and courage. . . . The price . . . [of survival] is a Lie.[9]

Such strategies enable Black Americans to persist, but not flourish, because they are contradictory to democracy. As Du Bois concludes, because Black Americans have no way to engage in the honest conversations and critiques that are essential to the creation and maintenance of an inclusive community, "all that makes life worth living" is currently marked "For White People Only."[10] This not only fosters bitterness among Black Americans, but also prevents the achievement of civic equality, which is crucial for democracy properly understood.

Following Du Bois, we contend that an expanded semantics of racism is necessary for the kinds of honest, in-depth conversations that build, maintain, and strengthen community as well as foster recognition of the right of diversity. Sometimes, such community-building occurs through the straightforward recognition and acceptance of people as co-members with input to give; other times, it involves finding new ways to talk to the people who are already within our communities. Given the history of the United States, which in large part is the ongoing, dynamic disaster of racism, expanding racial semantics is one way (among many!) to help bring about a robust democracy for all. Americans must be able to have "honest and earnest" conversations about race-based situations, injustice, and oppression, if they are going to achieve the attractive democratic vision that Du Bois sets out for the country. On this interpretation, what Du Bois provides for the United States is a theory of democratic development; as Elvira Basevich writes, through his commitment to democratic agency as building inclusive communities that recognize all members as sources of moral value and interpretation, Du Bois "maps the democratic transition *to* an ideally just society *from* a nonideal starting point, affirming that, historically, [B]lack political actors play a vital role imagining and guiding these transitions in US history."[11]

Moving from an illiberal white supremacist society premised on the social and political exclusion of Black Americans to civic equality and inclusivity is a tall order; yet it is one that Du Bois thinks can occur. When sub-communities within the society, such as civic and social associations, are formed that develop and protect democratic agency, they "ultimately contribute to reshaping the polity . . . on the free and equal terms that ideal-theory liberalism prizes."[12] At first glance, though, this might look like a chicken-and-egg problem. We need inclusive communities that recognize the right of diversity to have the difficult (racial and otherwise) conversations that are emblematic of Du Boisian democracy, and we need to have such conversations in order to build and maintain those inclusive communities. It is admittedly tricky; but this is why we advocate for starting with an expanded semantics of racism. (Du Bois himself calls for not only honest and earnest critique and conversation, but also banning redlining and promoting economic, educative, and artistic integration, among other strategies.)[13] Rather than think of it as a chicken-and-egg issue, instead think about a symbiotic relationship. It builds on itself, and pulls resources from other arenas too, to produce pockets of democratic community that can then spread outwards, until the entire political community can be rightly viewed as a Du Boisian democracy. This is grassroots organizing to create democracy.

The example that Du Bois gives of a civic association engaging in this process is the Black church. As Basevich puts it, interpreting Du Bois, "the [B]lack church did not simply encourage democratic discussion, it actualized [B]lack moral equality . . . [it] shouldered the responsibility of *enacting* the privileges morally appropriate to citizenship."[14] Via this creation of a pocket of democratic community, the Black church was able to legitimate certain norms of inclusivity and critique, and so call for improved public infrastructure and redistributions of social and political power, which "are developments from which *all* citizens benefit."[15] For example, the establishment of public school systems in the American South was first championed by the postbellum Black church, and only then taken up more broadly as a general political demand by the relevant white communities.[16] Part of Du Boisian democracy is democratic deliberation, which can only take place within conversational spaces where people are recognized as peers. You can't have an honest conversation about what to do if either party is afraid or unable to speak, for whatever reason. For Du Bois, the political circumstances are such that Black Americans have to create these conversational spaces themselves first, and then spread them outwards to transition the society toward a more fully democratic system. For this democratic transition to occur in the contemporary United States, an expanded semantics of racism is essential.

The existence of Historically Black Colleges and Universities (HBCUs) underscores the importance of Black spaces and institutions where Du Boisian democracy can be fostered. Recently, there has been a resurgence (or, perhaps, emergence) of support from governmental agencies, public

corporations, and private trusts that seems to recognize the importance of
these institutions not only for Black America, but also for the United States
as a whole. This support has come via historic federal HBCU-specific funding, a number of Presidential Executive Orders aimed at improving the
infrastructure and capacities of HBCUs, and many substantial philanthropic
donations, the most notable of which was MacKenzie Scott's series of donations over a four-month span in 2020 that totaled roughly $4.2 billion (though
not all of Scott's funding was specifically designated for HBCUs).[17] This
movement to support HBCUs as bastions of democratic equality is in line
with the arguments that Eddie S. Glaude Jr. makes regarding Black America
and its institutions in his 2017 book *Democracy in Black: How Race Still
Enslaves the American Soul.*[18] Following Du Bois, Glaude Jr. says that Black
institutions, such as Black newspapers, the Black church, Black social clubs,
Black masonic orders, fraternities, and sororities, and Black colleges and
universities are not *part* of Black America, they *are* Black America.[19] These
institutions have served, and continue to serve, as the life force of communities under continuous racial assault and provide services in lieu of the government's failure to extend the full benefits of citizenship to Black people. (For
example, think about the Black Panthers' breakfast programs, health clinics,
and tutoring programs.)

Focusing this discussion specifically on HBCUs and their role in fostering
Du Boisian democracy, HBCUs are spaces where groups of students and professionals are able to band together to identify interpersonal and institutional
problems that differentially affect Black Americans and work to bring about
real change. HBCUs afford Black Americans

> spaces to deliberate, to think, to organize—to breathe. They are (or were) key
> sites for [B]lack democratic life, especially in a country where [B]lack lives
> aren't as valued as other people's lives. They provided the elbow room to
> challenge white supremacy. But more than that, they comprised a safety net
> or backstop for [B]lack Americans living in a society defined by the value
> gap.[20]

Each of these components is essential to the creation of conversational
spaces, community, and Du Boisian democracy. Furthermore, we can see
evidence that this kind of grassroots cultivation of pockets of democracy in
HBCUs leads to democratic osmosis (exactly as Du Bois predicted). Look to
the White House and the now-current Biden administration—Kamala Harris,
a graduate of Howard University, is the current vice president of the United
States. Needless to say, this is an instance where a graduate of an HBCU,
a product of (likely numerous) Black institutions, is directly involved with
shaping American democracy at the highest levels.

Du Bois frames the role of Black political actors in the United States as that of creating civic equality through creating spaces for democratic agency. As he notes, though, this places the burden of creating a truly democratic politics disproportionately on Black shoulders.[21] This might strike some readers as deeply unfair—as philosopher Juliet Hooker notes, "taking seriously the idea . . . of democratic repair for [B]lack citizens means recognizing that responsibility for racial justice does not lie primarily with those who have already suffered the lion's share of the losses inflicted by racism."[22] This is undoubtedly true. Yet, insofar as the goal is to attain democratic justice for Black Americans, we may have to move beyond responsibility and considerations of what is fair, to an extent, and consider pragmatically what is likely to work. To be sure, Hooker is correct that we must *not* cast Du Boisian democracy as a kind of democratic exemplarity that is to be expected of Black Americans; rather, we must instead understand Du Boisian democracy as an aspiration to be worked toward by all members of the society. We maintain that part of achieving this goal is expanding our semantics so that we can have earnest, difficult conversations about the dynamic disaster of racism in American society. These conversations are necessary to creating robust democratic communities at all levels.

WORKING TOWARD JUSTICE

At this point, you might object that democracy is not what we should be aiming for. Perhaps liberal democracies are inherently white supremacist, and there is no saving them. As Charles Mills argues, the actual world in which we live is one predicated on a history of racial domination. It is woven through the formation of contemporary liberal democratic states, despite ahistorical social contract theories which uphold ideals of equality, liberty, and fundamental human rights.[23] Although Mills himself remains committed to the liberal democratic project—he describes his view as a Black radical liberalism[24]—other scholars have pushed further, arguing that racial justice requires moving away from democratic liberalism. This substantive debate is beyond the scope of our project here.[25] We maintain that even if the implementation of democracy is not an appropriate end, given its history and subsequent characteristics, the achievement of justice more broadly is a goal worth striving for. And it is one that requires an expanded semantics of racism, beyond the false trinary of racist/not racist/antiracist.

This leads immediately to the question of how to conceive of justice more broadly. We follow Iris Marion Young, who explicitly extends her understanding of justice beyond questions of distribution and rights. As she puts it, "justice means the elimination of institutionalized domination and oppression."[26] Justice is a matter of social practices and culture, as well as decision-making procedures regarding institutional norms and rules. It "covers everything political in this sense . . . some of these claims [about justice] involve distributions [and rights], but many also refer to other ways in which social institutions inhibit or liberate persons."[27] Young understands social institutions broadly, to include "all aspects of institutional organization, public action, social practices and habits, and cultural meanings insofar as they are potentially subject to collective evaluation and decision making."[28] These social connections, in which we are all embedded and to which we all contribute, can be instruments of domination and oppression (injustice), or of liberation and development (justice). To work toward justice is to work to bring about social practices, cultural meanings, and institutional conditions that enable and support, without compelling, the exercise of self-determination and self-development and "collective communication and cooperation."[29]

This way of thinking about justice and injustice is structural; as philosopher Robin Zheng interprets her, Young is primarily concerned with the ongoing social processes that form "the *unjust background conditions* against which ordinary actions occur, rather than specific actions" themselves.[30] What is it, then, that makes some individual action, such as wearing blackface, Judge Bruce Schroeder's cell phone ringtone playing "God Bless the USA" while he was presiding over the Kyle Rittenhouse murder trial, or Christine Caswell's calling the police on Boston Red Sox Hall-of-Famer Tommy Harper for looking at her while she was walking her dog, racially problematic in the United States? It is that the background social processes and practices of the society are themselves unjust, such that the action carries with it oppressive and dominating cultural meanings, and further cements those unjust processes and practices as accepted and normal ways of doing and thinking things, of organizing people's lives, perspectives, institutions, and communities. The perpetuation of structural injustice is fundamentally social. Thus, the move toward justice must be social as well.

To achieve justice equally enjoyed by all, all social processes and practices that are characterized by domination and oppression must change. Straightforwardly, it is not possible for such social processes to be changed or reformed by one person; this gives the impetus to work together. As Young puts it, "These processes can be altered only if many actors from diverse positions within the social structures work together to intervene in them to try to produce other outcomes."[31] This point is partially metaphysical—the *nature* of social processes and practices is such that they cannot be single-handedly changed by any one individual—and partially pragmatic. Given the social structural nature of injustice, many people are going to have to work together, practically speaking, to create real, sustained change. One white lady being nice to her Black neighbors isn't going to cut it, just like eating one salad isn't going to make you healthy. It's a good and necessary start, yes (depending on what kind of salad it is), but it's not sufficient to fix the problem. To do that, the white lady has to go deeper, and work with others to change the social structures of her society that make it accepted, in general, for white ladies to be standoffish, mean, and downright ugly to their Black neighbors.[32]

Now, why should the white lady do this? More broadly, why should anyone strive to move their society away from oppressive and dominating conditions and toward those social structures that enable and support self-determination, self-development, and collective communication and cooperation? Well, first and foremost because justice, intuitively, is of primary political importance. As one of the standout political philosophers of the twentieth century, John Rawls, states at the outset of *A Theory of Justice*, "Justice is the first virtue of social institutions, as truth is of systems of thought. A theory however elegant and economical must be rejected or revised if it is untrue; likewise laws and institutions no matter how efficient and well-arranged must be reformed or abolished if they are unjust. . . . Being first virtues of human activities, truth and justice are uncompromising."[33] If a society is not, in some broad sense, concerned with bringing about justice (however conceived), then it is difficult to see it as a political society at all. This is compatible with a society being *wrong* about what justice is. The Khmer Rouge, in their slaughter of two million Cambodians, embodied injustice;[34] but crucially, they *thought* they were bringing about justice. This is not to excuse the Khmer Rouge, but rather to draw out Rawls's point. However they conceive of it—rightly or wrongly—people in general care about justice, and making their societies more just.

Of course, some individuals within a society may not be particularly concerned with justice for a variety of reasons. Perhaps they are too busy, or they have other obligations with which they are primarily concerned, or they've never really thought about it, or they think they cannot do anything to make their society more just, or they think that their society is already pretty just, and so on. Most people with these sorts of reasons, when pressed, admit that they do *care* about justice—they just don't act on that caring for any number of reasons. More rarely, some individuals claim to not care about justice at all. Just as some people do not care about being moral, so too do some not care about their society being just. This is the longstanding "open question" of both moral and political philosophy. In ethics, it is "Why be moral?" In political philosophy, it is "Why be just?" In both cases, there is no satisfactory answer. To attempt to provide one here would take us too far afield; so, we limit our discussion to those who *are* concerned with bringing about a more just society. See chapter five for more on this claim.

If you care about justice, you should work to bring about a more just society. And more than that, Young argues that all people within a society have an obligation to change unjust social processes and practices, because everyone is responsible, in the sense of being *accountable*, for their existence. We are all embedded in these dominating and oppressive social processes and practices; we cannot help but maintain and perpetuate them, simply via living our lives. As Zheng argues, "Each of us is causally implicated in these injustices through the ineluctable everyday actions we perform to provide for ourselves and others: the very acts of feeding, clothing, sheltering, and caring oblige us to participate in globally exploitative structural processes" such as imperialism, marginalization, institutional violence and exclusion, and the like.[35] We shop at grocery stores, buy clothes for ourselves and others, attend sporting events and concerts, send our children to school, and the like. On the one hand, these are normal, everyday activities that are, considered in isolation, morally acceptable (absent special circumstances). But on the other hand, shopping at grocery stores furthers the exploitation of farm workers, buying clothes perpetuates the environmentally unsustainable and oppressive fashion industry, attending cultural activities and events supports the dominating and disempowering systems that produce professional athletes and artists, and sending children to school reinforces an educational system that systematically centers whiteness, erases the historical contributions of persons of color, and marginalizes current Black and brown students and educational professionals.

Now, for the most part, we are not to *blame* for structural injustice. It "makes up the very fabric of the current social world in which we are all enmeshed."[36] In many cases, even when we know we are participating in unjust social processes and practices, we cannot meaningfully do otherwise. We cannot simply stop eating, raising our children, and participating in social life. We operate under a series of institutional, social, and structural constraints. So, we are not *liable*—again, absent special circumstances—for the unjust social processes and practices that make up our society. Young is quite clear here: she writes, "[W]e should not be blamed or found at fault for the injustice we contribute to."[37] In other words, we should not be punished, nor should we feel guilty, for perpetuating the unjust background conditions of our society, because in most cases we could not freely exercise our moral agency to meaningfully act otherwise.[38]

However, we are causally connected to those unjust background conditions; we help maintain them, every day, through our myriad actions. Because of these roles that we play in social structural injustices, we are thereby accountable for working to change them. As Zheng interprets Young, "the individual must take up a portion of the collective burden of social transformation *because* the individual has, in the past, causally contributed to that unjust outcome."[39] This causal contribution, again, does not make the burden of blame appropriate—it makes no sense to bean-count, for the most part, to try to determine who, precisely, has done what and when. The overwhelming amount of injustice present, to which we all contribute, means that all of our slates are dirty.[40] It is thus appropriate to assign everyone the burden of transformation, of working to change our social processes and practices so that they are more just. As Zheng concludes, our accountability for the existence of ongoing structural injustice provides us with a particular set of political obligations: "As a result of our causal participation in unjust structures, we must take steps to communicate with each other, coordinate our actions, and publicly advocate for structural transformation."[41] We're all in a sinking boat—rather than sit and debate who made the hole or crack, everyone needs to grab a bucket and start bailing. What kind of bucket you need to grab is a further question, one we discuss in chapter six.[42]

People who care about justice, then, but fail to act for a variety of reasons, may be criticized for failing to uphold their political obligations to work toward justice. As Young says, although we are not blameworthy for the presence of unjust social processes and practices, we are accountable, and so "we can and should be *criticized* for not taking action [to try and rectify injustice], not taking enough action, taking ineffective action, or taking action that is counterproductive."[43] We must work to bring about more just social processes and practices, and crucially, we must engage in specific kinds of actions to do so—simply being nice to the neighbors isn't going to cut it. Neither, for that matter, is growing our own veggies, shopping only at secondhand stores, swearing off attending concerts where the roadies aren't paid a living wage, nor homeschooling our children, and so on. All of these actions help, of course, insofar as they have the potential to provide a cultural counterpoint to common unjust social practices.[44] But they do not discharge our political obligations to work toward justice. To meet those obligations, we must work together to try, in productive, effective ways, to bring about a transformation of our social processes and practices so that they enable and support self-determination, self-development, and collective communication and cooperation.

PRODUCTIVE AND EFFECTIVE ACTION AGAINST INJUSTICE

The nature of social processes and practices, as we discuss above, demands coordination to create real, sustained change. But that coordination to bring about justice cannot happen in a vacuum. To work together effectively and productively, people are going to have to communicate with each other to clarify what the problems of injustice are, where they lie, and how they might effectively tackle them. Otherwise, it is likely that people will work at cross-purposes or in isolation, and so fail to bring about meaningful change. This is not to say that a clearly defined set of goals, and outlined tactics for achieving those goals, guarantees success, as any committee member, or military professional, can tell you. Even the best-laid plans can fail to materialize. But communicating about those plans as clearly as possible is certainly a good, and possibly a necessary, start!

Communication is key to bringing about justice more equally enjoyed by all. However, in the United States, communication about racism and racial injustice often fails, in part due to the semantic false trinary of racist/not racist/antiracist.[45] So long as the common view of racism in the United States is that it is an individual, character-based flaw, the conversations that Young calls for are practically impossible. We need an expanded semantics of racism to have the kinds of conversations that are necessary to take productive, effective, coordinated action against structural injustice. Justice requires that we not only coordinate, and thus communicate, but also that we communicate in the right kinds of ways about what is just and unjust in society. We cannot communicate about the dynamic disaster of racism without an expanded semantics of racism which enables people to recognize a) that racially unjust social processes and practices exist, b) that they are accountable for such racial injustices, but not blameworthy (except in special cases where clear lines of fault and liability can be drawn), and c) that this accountability generates a political obligation to take coordinated action to attempt to bring about the relevant social transformations.

As Young reiterates, we should not be blamed if our efforts to bring about justice fail. However, we are appropriately criticized if we do not even try, or if we try in ways that we know will likely be ineffective and unproductive. Taking up an expanded semantics of racism—that moves beyond the false trinary—is to attempt to communicate properly with others in US society about the nature of racially unsettling situations, which is the first step in generating cooperation to bring about transformative change. For example, Jen cares about justice. But if she cannot see what the problem is with using the racially derogatory word "thug" because she does not have the proper conceptual-semantic resources, and if Leland cannot get her to see the problem without triggering her white fragility because he does not have an expanded semantics to draw on, then she is not able to see what justice demands of her—she is not able to recognize that she ought to stop using the word, and coordinate with others to change the unjust background conditions of her society that make the use of the word "thug" both racially derogatory and common. To leverage Jen's caring about justice into helpful action for justice, we need a semantic shift. Such a shift would help to enable the productive, effective conversations about racial injustice that are part and parcel of the work of coordinating to create more emancipatory social practices and relieve the dynamic disaster of racism.

Of course, the semantic shift we describe, to an expanded, non-character-based spectrum of language around racism, is not the only work that needs doing to move toward justice. But it is a critical step. We need to have the tough conversations, to stage an intervention, as cultural critic, theorist, and activist Brittney Cooper puts it, to call "America out on her bullshit about racism, sexism, classism, homophobia, and a bunch of other stuff."[46] As she says, "America needs a homegirl intervention in the worst way . . . with eloquent rage."[47] To do this in an effective and productive way, as we are obliged to do, we need to change our language, so that we can keep talking to each other in the right kinds of ways, to have a chance of bringing about justice more equally enjoyed by all.

NOTES

1. "Covers Her Face With Both Hands," from the Penguin publication *The Gift: Poems of Hafiz* by Daniel Ladinsky, copyright 1999 and used with permission.

2. Charles W. Mills, *The Racial Contract* (Ithaca, NY: Cornell University Press, 1997).

3. Tom Christiano and Sameer Bajaj, "Democracy," *The Stanford Encyclopedia of Philosophy*, Fall 2021.

4. Sam Levine and Ankita Rao, "In 2013 the Supreme Court Gutted Voting Rights—How has it Changed the US?" *The Guardian*, June 25, 2020.

5. Du Bois, W. E. B., *The Souls of Black Folk* (New York: Taylor & Francis, 2004).

6. Du Bois, W. E. B., "The Immediate Problem of the American Negro," *The Crisis* 9, no. 6 (1915): n.p.

7. Du Bois, W. E. B., *The Souls of Black Folk*, ch. 3.

8. Du Bois, W. E. B., *The Souls of Black Folk*, 25.

9. Du Bois, W. E. B., *The Souls of Black Folk*, 109.

10. Du Bois, W. E. B., *The Souls of Black Folk*, 110.

11. Elvira Basevich, "W. E. B. Du Bois's Critique of American Democracy during the Jim Crow Era: On the Limitations of Rawls and Honneth," *The Journal of Political Philosophy* 27, no. 3 (2019): 323.

12. Basevich, "W. E. B. Du Bois's Critique of American Democracy during the Jim Crow Era: On the Limitations of Rawls and Honneth," 323.

13. Du Bois, W. E. B., *The Souls of Black Folk.*

14. Basevich, "W. E. B. Du Bois's Critique of American Democracy during the Jim Crow Era: On the Limitations of Rawls and Honneth," 332–33.

15. Basevich, "W. E. B. Du Bois's Critique of American Democracy during the Jim Crow Era: On the Limitations of Rawls and Honneth," 333.

16. Du Bois, W. E. B., *Black Reconstruction* (New York: Free Press, 1992), 638.

17. Laurel Wamsley, "MacKenzie Scott has Donated More than $4 Billion in Last 4 Months," *NPR,* December 16, 2020.

18. We discuss Glaude Jr.'s book in more depth in chapter three. Eddie S. Glaude Jr., *Democracy in Black: How Race Still Enslaves the American Soul* (New York: Broadway Books, 2017).

19. Glaude Jr., *Democracy in Black: How Race Still Enslaves the American Soul,* ch. 6.

20. Glaude Jr., *Democracy in Black: How Race Still Enslaves the American Soul,* 126.

21. Alexander Livingston, "The Cost of Liberty: Sacrifice and Survival in Du Bois's John Brown," in *A Political Companion to W.E.B. Du Bois*, ed. Nick Bromell (Lexington: University Press of Kentucky, 2018), 207–40.

22. Juliet Hooker, "Black Lives Matter and the Paradoxes of U.S. Black Politics: From Democratic Sacrifice to Democratic Repair," *Political Theory* 44, no. 4 (2016): 465.

23. Mills, *The Racial Contract*, ch. 1.

24. Daniel Steinmetz-Jenkins, "Charles Mills Thinks Liberalism Still has a Chance," *The Nation,* January 28, 2021.

25. For more regarding our views on democracy, liberalism, and radical politics, see Leland Harper, ed., *The Crisis of American Democracy: Essays on a Failing Institution* (Wilmington, DE: Vernon Press, 2022); Jennifer Kling and Megan Mitchell, *The Philosophy of Protest: Fighting for Justice without Going to War* (Lanham, MD: Rowman & Littlefield International, 2021).

26. Iris Marion Young, *Justice and the Politics of Difference* (New Jersey: Princeton University Press, 1990), 15.

27. Young, *Justice and the Politics of Difference*, 34.

28. Young, *Justice and the Politics of Difference*, 34.

29. Young, *Justice and the Politics of Difference*, 39.

30. Robin Zheng, "What Kind of Responsibility do we have for Fighting Injustice? A Moral-Theoretic Perspective on the Social Connections Model," *Critical Horizons* 20, no. 2 (2019): 111, emphasis in original.

31. Iris Marion Young, *Responsibility for Justice* (Oxford: Oxford University Press, 2011), 112.

32. It is worth noting that some of this work is being done in the United States currently with the introduction of the negative "Karen" figure into social consciousness. The generalized condemnation aimed at white women who act like "Karens" in a variety of class-based situations and race-based situations is quite vocal and, so far, sustained: it may be enough to change some of the social practices of white women, particularly those with certain sorts of class and race privileges (e.g., the white women who formed the Wall of Moms during the 2020 Portland, Oregon, protests were called

"anti-Karens"). Ashitha Nagesh, "What Exactly is a 'Karen' and Where did the Meme Come from?" *BBC,* July 31, 2020. For a broader and more in-depth look at the complexities of the interplay between white well-intentioned interpersonal interactions and changing social practices, see Robin DiAngelo, *Nice Racism: How Progressive White People Perpetuate Racial Harm* (Boston, MA: Beacon Press, 2021).

33. John Rawls, *A Theory of Justice, Revised Edition* (Cambridge, MA: Belknap Press, 1999), 3–4.

34. Staff, "Khmer Rouge: Cambodia's Years of Brutality," *BBC,* November 16, 2018.

35. Zheng, "What Kind of Responsibility do we have for Fighting Injustice? A Moral-Theoretic Perspective on the Social Connections Model," 111.

36. Zheng, "What Kind of Responsibility do we have for Fighting Injustice? A Moral-Theoretic Perspective on the Social Connections Model," 111.

37. Young, *Responsibility for Justice*, 144.

38. As Zheng notes, though, there may be some cases where powerful agents could have freely and meaningfully acted otherwise to thwart structural injustice, and in such cases, it may be appropriate to blame, punish, hold them liable, etc. Zheng, "What Kind of Responsibility do we have for Fighting Injustice? A Moral-Theoretic Perspective on the Social Connections Model," fn 31 and fn 40.

39. Zheng, "What Kind of Responsibility do we have for Fighting Injustice? A Moral-Theoretic Perspective on the Social Connections Model," 118, emphasis in original.

40. You might be tempted to tack on a rider here, to say that everyone's slate is dirty "to varying degrees." Young, and Zheng when interpreting Young, want to get away from this kind of "degree" or "amount" talk. We discuss this more in chapter six.

41. Zheng, "What Kind of Responsibility do we have for Fighting Injustice? A Moral-Theoretic Perspective on the Social Connections Model," 117.

42. Young would say that once we're to safety, we can look to assign blame for the creation of the hole or crack. But in the unjust meantime, we need to focus on bailing, not blaming.

43. Young, *Responsibility for Justice*, 144, emphasis in original.

44. For more on how the existence of cultural counterpoints can open up new social possibilities, see Sally Haslanger, "What is a Social Practice?" *Royal Institute of Philosophy Supplement* 82 (2018), 242.

45. For our argument for this claim, see chapter two.

46. Brittney Cooper, *Eloquent Rage* (New York: St. Martins Press, 2018), 5.

47. Cooper, *Eloquent Rage*, 5–6.

Chapter Five

Aaron Bailey • Aaron Campbell • Aiyana Mo'Nay Stanley-Jones • Akai Kareem Gurley • Alberta Spruill • Alesia Thomas • Alfred Olango • Alonzo Ashley • Alton Sterling • Amadou Diallo • Andre Maurice Hill • Andy Lopez • Angelo "AJ" Crooms • Angelo Quinto • Anton Milbert LaRue Black • Antwon Rose Jr. • Arthur Miller Jr. • Atatiana Koquice Jefferson • Barrington "BJ" Williams • Barry Gene Evans • Bettie "Betty Boo" Jones • Bijan Ghaisar • Botham Shem Jean • Brendon K. Glenn • Breonna Taylor • Carlos Alcis • Carlos Carson • Casey Christopher Goodson Jr. • Chad Robertson • Charleena Chavon Lyles • Fetus of Charleena Chavon Lyles • Charles "Chop" Roundtree Jr. • Chavis Carter • Chinedu Okobi • Clinton R. Allen • Corey Lamar Jones • Daniel T. Prude • Dannette "Strawberry" Daniels • Danroy "DJ" Henry Jr. • Dante Parker • Dante' Lamar Price • Darnisha Diana Harris • Daunte Demetrius Wright • David McAtee • DeAunta Terrel Farrow • Deborah Danner • Dennis Plowden Jr. • Derek Williams • Derrick Jones • Dijon Durand Kizzee • Dontre Hamilton • Dreasjon "Sean" Reed • Earl Murray • Eleanor Bumpers • Elijah McClain • Emantic "EJ" Fitzgerald Bradford Jr. • Eric Courtney Harris • Eric Garner • Ervin Lee Jefferson III • Eula Mae Love • Ezell Ford • Frankie Ann Perkins • Freddie Carlos Gray Jr. • Gabriella Monique Nevarez • George Perry Floyd • Gregory Lloyd Edwards • Henry "Ace" Glover • Henry Dumas • India Kager • Jamaal Moore Sr. • Jamar O'Neal Clark • James B. Brissette Jr. • James Earl Green • Janisha Fonville • Javier Ambler • Jerame C. Reid • Jeremy "Bam Bam" McDole • Jersey K. Green • John Crawford III • John Elliot Neville • Johnnie Kamahi Warren • Jonathan Dwayne Price • Jonathan Ferrell • Jordan Baker • Jordan Edwards • Joseph Curtis Mann • Kathryn Johnston • Kayla Moore • Kendra Sarie James • Kendrec McDade • Kenneth Chamberlain Sr. • Kimani "KiKi" Gray • Kiwane Carrington • Korryn Gaines • Kyam Livingston •

Larry Eugene Jackson Jr. • LaTanya Haggerty • Malcolm Ferguson • Malissa Williams • Manual Levi Loggins Jr. • Manuel "Mannie" Elijah Ellis • Marcellis Stinnette • Margaret LaVerne Mitchell • Marvin David Scott III • Mary Mitchell • McKenzie J. Cochran • Meagan Hockaday • Michael Brent Charles Ramos • Michael Brown Jr. • Michael Jerome Stewart • Miriam Iris Carey • Mya Shawatza Hall • Natasha McKenna • Nehemiah Lazar Dillard • Nelson Martinez Mendez • Nicholas Heyward Jr. • Noel Palanco • Orlando Barlow • Oscar Grant III • Ousmane Zongo • Patrick Lynn Warren Sr. • Patrick Moses Dorismond • Philando Castile • Phillip Gregory White • Phillip Lafayette Gibbs • Prince Carmen Jones Jr. • Quintonio LeGrier • Raheim Brown, Jr. • Ramarley Graham • Randolph Evans • Raymond Luther Allen Jr. • Rayshard Brooks • Reginald Doucet • Rekia Boyd • Reynaldo Cuevas • Rita Lloyd • Ronald Beasley • Ronald Curtis Madison • Ronald Greene • Rumain Brisbon • Saheed Vassell • Samuel Vincent DuBose • Sandra Bland • Sean Bell • Shantel Davis • Sharmel T. Edwards • Shelly Marie Frey • Shem Walker • Shereese Francis • Sincere Pierce • Stephon Alonzo Clark • Sterling Lapree Higgins • Steven Eugene Washington • Tamir Rice • Tamon Robinson • Tanisha N. Anderson • Tarika Wilson • Terence Crutcher • Terrence LeDell Sterling • Timothy DeWayne Thomas Jr. • Timothy Russell • Timothy Stansbury, Jr. • Tony "Tony the Tiger" McDade • Tony Terrell Robinson, Jr. • Tyisha Shenee Miller • Tyree Woodson • Victor Steen • Victor White III • Vincent "Vinny" M. Belmonte • Walter Lamar Scott • Wendell James Allen • William Howard Green • Yvette Smith • Yvonne Smallwood

Chapter Six

Conversations

> *. . . after much frustration trying to determine whether or not the yet-to-be-had conversation is indeed about race, somebody gives up and walks away, leaving the original issue untouched.*
>
> —Ijeoma Oluo[1]

It is hard to have the kinds of conversations about racial injustice and oppression that are required for the United States, as a society, to make progress toward either Du Boisian democracy or justice more broadly construed. The first step is to ensure that people who care about democracy or justice have the proper language for such conversations to possibly occur—hence, our conclusion that we need an expanded semantics of racism. The second step is to consider the communicative context more broadly, to discern the other dialogic constraints that hold on different parties who are engaging in this kind of communication. We want these conversations to continue in the right kinds of ways, that is, the kinds of ways that are conducive to bringing about democratic agency and transforming social processes and practices to be more just. So, this chapter focuses first on the question of what else is required of interlocuters, communicatively speaking, in order to produce this result. Then, we discuss in depth why people ought to be motivated to accept these dialogic constraints, as well as our proposed semantic shift.

DIALOGIC CONSTRAINTS

Communication, to occur at all, must meet a series of conditions. Many of these are straightforward, but others, less so. When parties enter into communication, they accept certain communicative, or dialogic, norms as part of the exchange. For instance, people must at least try to hear and understand what others are saying, and they must try to make their own points clear. If they don't make those efforts, it is hard to see them as communicating at all. There are a variety of modes of communication, of course—clarity does not require earnestness (think about getting your point across with humor rather than a rant), and hearing and understanding may not demand full attention at any given time (think about the child who does better in school when they can doodle while listening to a lecture). Regardless of communicative modes, the point is that those who would engage in communication at all have to meet a series of dialogic conditions. And for people who want to engage in specific kinds of communication, such as communication about racism in the contemporary United States, there are specific further dialogic constraints that apply.

In our view, the relevant conversations about racism (on which we've been focused throughout the book) are an exercise of our political responsibility not simply to speak out publicly against injustice, but to do so in an effort to motivate others to help improve the situation. Given this obligation, not any kind of communication will do. We discuss each constraint that holds on these kinds of conversations in turn. That people must convey condemnation while motivating others means, at a minimum, they must attend to the context of their communication. They must analyze the capacities of their audience, as well as attend to their own wellbeing and the wellbeing of other members of marginalized groups. Intention versus impact is key here! Meanwhile, their interlocutors must try to hear and understand what is being said to them— they must strive to not be so fragile and defensive that they leave the "original issue untouched," as social theorist and author Ijeoma Oluo puts it.[2] These duties are not unique to conversations about racism, of course, although that is our focus here—they also apply to conversations about other oppressive and dominating social structures (such as misogyny, classism, ableism, and heteronormativity) as well.

Analyzing the Communicative Context

In chapter two, we emphasized, following Robin DiAngelo, that most white people in the US struggle to discuss structural racism without engaging in defensive conversational maneuvers that shut the conversation down before it can really begin. We concluded that this white fragility is due at least in part to our impoverished, character-based semantics of racism. Hence, our argument for a semantic shift—we need more and better language with which to discuss racially problematic situations, language which is not closely linked in people's minds to good and bad character traits. Following this, the person attempting to communicate about the presence of structural racism in the United States, and the ways in which a particular interpersonal incident is race-based because of that overarching racism, must attempt to remain aware of this communicative context and so use either our suggested new term (see chapter seven) or relevantly similar language.

Frustratingly, many white people in the United States are like children when it comes to these conversations—they are inexperienced in communicating maturely about racism. As Oluo, DiAngelo, and others point out, the urge to avoid the conversation, in whatever way is available, is strong. Think of a child who physically runs away when they break a glass. White adults might not physically run away when they are called into a discussion about a race-based incident, but they are likely to intellectually or emotionally withdraw. The person attempting to communicate with them should bear this in mind, and, to the extent that they feel able, engage in communicative strategies to "stop the run." This analysis of the communicative context, in particular the capacities of the audience, leads to the recognition that these conversations, if they are to be productive, need to be more like therapy sessions, or at the least call ins, rather than call outs. The right kinds of conversations about racism are, in the first instance, the ones that don't get shut down right off the bat.

Importantly, our point here is not simply pragmatic. While call ins are likely to be more effective than call outs, for reasons we discuss in a moment, that is not the only reason for managing such conversations in this way. As we argued in chapter four, the responsibility that most US Americans bear for racism is not liability, but accountability; thus, blaming them—which is what call outs do—is not, in most cases, appropriate. Becky cannot control that, in the United States, social processes and practices around beauty standards make it the case that commenting on a Black person's hairstyle, as a white woman, is a racially charged act. It may be appropriate to criticize Becky for not knowing this (depending on other factors), or for failing to work with others to change the unjust background conditions that make this true, but it is inappropriate, in most cases, to straightforwardly morally blame her. More appropriate is to inform her that her actions are racially insensitive, remind her that she is accountable for the dynamic disaster that is US racism, and call on her to work with others to bring about needed changes. Basically, we're saying, "Becky, you're not a bad person—you've just got to get your shit together." As social theorist, educator, and author Beverly Tatum puts it, a person might truthfully say to Becky, "It [racism] is not our fault, but it is our responsibility to interrupt this cycle."[3]

The goal of these conversations is to steer people toward being account-able and changing, rather than feeling guilty and shutting down. In this vein, using an expanded semantics that explicitly focuses on the person's epistemic situation—that is, their lack of knowledge or understanding—rather than their moral character, is less likely to trigger guilt and/or shame and ensuing defensiveness. The exception to this might be academics, who sometimes care much more about their epistemic situation than their character. It is easy to imagine a professor saying, "Impugn my character all you want, but don't tell me I'm ignorant!" However, our suspicion is that this response is somewhat unique to those whose business is knowledge. In the ordinary course of things, one main reason why conversations about racism in the United States get derailed is because white people take them to be conversations about their morality, not their knowledge and understanding or lack thereof. Thus, redirecting these conversations, via the use of new linguistic terminology, away from morality and toward the introduction of new knowledge and understandings is likely to enable them to continue without the person in question literally or metaphorically walking away.

But of course, just because it is less likely to make the person being communicated with shut down, does not mean that our epistemically focused, expanded semantics of racism is foolproof. There is no guarantee that using such language will always lead to the kinds of conversations that are needed to bring about justice more equally enjoyed by all. Some people are equally defensive of their character *and* their epistemic situation. Consider the January 18, 2021, introduction by then–US president Trump of the 1776 Project to counteract the 1619 Project. The 1619 Project reframes the history of the United States by arguing that the nation started in 1619, with the arrival of the first enslaved persons from Africa onto North American shores, rather than with the US Declaration of Independence, which was signed in 1776. It does not make any explicit moral claims, but rather is an attempt to put the "contributions of [B]lack Americans at the very center of our national narrative."[4] The 1776 Project, by contrast, claims to be the "definitive chronicle of the American founding," put together explicitly as a "rebuttal of reckless 're-education' attempts that seek to reframe American history."[5] This is a clear case of Trump and his associates responding badly to a challenge to their epistemic situation. Perhaps they took The 1619 Project as a challenge to their character, and that explains their response; or perhaps they simply did not like being challenged epistemically. Regardless, the point is that expanding our semantics is not a guaranteed cure-all. Conversation is always a two-way street; there will inevitably be a subset of people who respond badly to being corrected, regardless of whether that correction takes a moral or an epistemological tone. It is helpful here to recall that we are not politically obliged to *succeed* in having the right kinds of conversations; we are simply obliged to *try*, as best we can, using the various tools at our disposal. Given the existing communicative context in the United States, an expanded semantics of racism is one such tool.

An additional communicative strategy, as we mentioned above, that arises from an analysis of the communicative context is thinking about these conversations as a kind of therapeutic exercise, as a calling in rather than a calling out. While such "naming and shaming" can sometimes be appropriate, in cases where the individual is liable, it is often not actually morally appropriate—although it might make the caller feel good—and in many cases is unlikely to have the desired effect of motivating justice-oriented changes in the callee's subsequent actions. As philosopher Kimberley Brownlee writes, discussing communicating in protest (and what are these conversations, if not a kind of protest against injustice), we must "consider whether our chosen means of communication—words, actions, images, body movements, facial expressions—and modes of communication—aggressively, violently, collectively, supportively—are likely to foster understanding in a way that is compatible" with continued and productive dialogue.[6] The intention is to communicate toward collective action for justice. Given that intention, we have a communicative responsibility to work with the capacities of our audience. To do this is to attempt to treat them as possible co-members in a Du Boisian democratic community—rather than abandoning them as lost causes, or subjecting them to a monologue of their faults, we invite them into a dialogue that presumes at the outset that they are able to, with some assistance, achieve understanding about the dynamic disaster of racism in the United States, and be motivated to organize for change.[7]

To be clear, some people are committed to misunderstanding others when they attempt to discuss racism. There is a nugget of truth to Upton Sinclair's quip that "It is difficult to get a man to understand something, when his salary depends upon his not understanding it."[8] For those who are determined to uphold the United States as a white supremacist society for economic, ideological, or other reasons, no amount of therapeutic discussion is likely to bring awareness and comprehension and motivate engagement in collective efforts to transform the United States into a democratic, just society. See Mitch McConnell. But for others, who are not so committed, something akin to a call in, or therapeutic dialogue, which makes use of an expanded semantics to discuss race-based situations, processes, practices, and structures, may be more successful. As Rutgers University Director of Faculty Diversity Education and Outreach Crystal Bedley argues, this "clueless, but well-intentioned" group "is the largest by far."[9] Their epistemic situation is such, and their morality is such, that they "are willing to put in the effort, so long as the effort is fed to them in easy to digest pieces."[10] So, she concludes, her strategy is to be "attentive to the ways [she] might antagonize and instead express appreciation for their budding commitment . . . [to] guide the transition from being well-intentioned to allyship, and grow the collective effort needed to create sustained change."[11] This strategy is both pragmatic and, following Iris Marion Young (see chapter four), mostly morally apt.

You might worry that these dialogic constraints, as we have discussed them so far, inexorably lead to putting the burden on those who are already oppressed to explain the truth of the dynamic disaster of racism to white people. In response, it is first important to point out that the political responsibility to take collective action toward justice holds for all US nationals. This is what grounds the obligation to, among other things, have the kinds of conversations about racism, democracy, and justice that are necessary to bring about and coordinate such collective action. Everyone in US society is obliged to have these conversations—but only to the extent that they are able. When people are genuinely not able to have these conversations, which could occur for a variety of reasons, including their own wellbeing and the wellbeing of others, then they are not obliged to do so. And in general, people's ability to have difficult conversations can vary over time—some days, smashing through misconceptions and ignorance is our jam, and other days, we just can't. Coordinating to transform social processes and practices to be more liberatory is a long game; thus, attending to our own wellbeing, as well as the wellbeing of others in the fight with us, is crucial to success. Better to wait and converse another day, than communicate when you're not in the right headspace to do so, and risk real mental and emotional harm to yourself and others.

Second, a full analysis of the communicative context generates a defeater to the obligation to have such conversations. When the context is such that engaging in a conversation about structural racism and its instantiation in an interpersonal incident is likely to increase the oppression and domination that a person faces, as is often true for Black Americans, then the obligation to have that conversation is eclipsed. Crucially, only Black Americans can make this decision—their lived experience enables them to know, better than any outside onlooker, when conversations about race-based incidents are likely to be detrimental to their, and others', prospects and likelihood of living a flourishing life. As author and social critic James Baldwin puts it, "it is the Black condition . . . which informs us concerning white people . . . and power."[12] Black Americans know when initiating a conversation about a race-based incident is in their and their fellows' interests, and when it is not, because they understand the operation of white power and privilege at play in the contemporary United States. To speak bluntly, nobody understands white Americans like Black Americans. As Du Bois puts the point lyrically:

> Of them [white folk] I am singularly clairvoyant. I see in and through them. I view them from unusual points of vantage. Not as a foreigner do I come, for I am native, not foreign, bone of their thought and flesh of their language. Mine

is not the knowledge of the traveler or the colonial composite of dear memories, words and wonder. Nor yet is my knowledge that which servants have of masters, or mass of class, or capitalist of artisan. Rather I see these souls undressed and from the back and side. I see the working of their entrails. I know their thoughts and they know that I know. This knowledge makes them now embarrassed, now furious. They deny my right to live and be and call me misbirth! My word is to them mere bitterness and my soul, pessimism. And yet as they preach and strut and shout and threaten, crouching as they clutch at rags of facts and fancies to hide their nakedness, they go twisting, flying by my tired eyes and I see them ever stripped,—ugly, human.[13]

Part of living under conditions of oppression and domination is that political responsibilities are context-sensitive; no one has an obligation to do, in any particular case, that which will manifestly lead to their increased oppression and domination. So, if speaking to a white co-worker about the racially insensitive joke they made is likely to lead to a Black American's being marginalized and further exploited while at work, then her political obligation to have that conversation is defeated—she need not do so. Of course, if she wants to do so, then she certainly may, and we might well applaud her; but courage takes many forms, and sometimes the better part of valor is protecting oneself, and other members of the Black American community, for another day and another circumstance. As the Black lesbian feminists of the Combahee River Collective put it in their 1977 manifesto, "We do not want to mess over people in the name of politics."[14] The political ends do not always justify the means, when what is at stake is Black Americans' ability to survive and flourish in conditions of oppression and domination.

White Americans, by contrast, do not have access to this defeater. Because white Americans are not subject to racist domination and oppression, their political responsibility to communicate toward collective action, and thus their obligation to have the right kinds of conversations, always holds. Although this political responsibility can be in tension with their moral obligations toward themselves and others (e.g., the duties to attend to well-being we mentioned above), it is not defeated by the political context in which they live. When David, who is white, urges his neighborhood association to put up "Black Lives Matter" signs, that conversation—however difficult it may be—does not put David in any real danger of being oppressed by his fellows. They may ignore or deride him, but his attempts, assuming they meet the dialogic constraints we have outlined here, are politically obligatory and not eclipsed by the nature of his society's unjust background conditions. So, while the political obligation to engage in collective, transformative efforts toward justice falls on all US nationals, it falls especially onto white US nationals, rather than Black US nationals, who already bear the burden of living in a racially oppressive society.

Importantly, for those who are racially ambiguous, the situation varies: an analysis of the communicative context, for them, will include an analysis of whether and how they are being racialized, which then imposes differential dialogic constraints. Sometimes, the communicative context will be such that they are more likely to be heard, given the capacities of their audience. Colorism is a feature of antiBlack racism in the United States; thus, those with a lighter skin tone, that is, those who could be racialized in different ways depending on the particulars of the situation, are perhaps more likely to be trusted and listened to by clueless but (hopefully!) well-intentioned whites. There are things about racism that light-skinned comedian Trevor Noah can say that darker-skinned Black Americans cannot say without threat of reprisal.[15] But still, because of mixed-race persons' racially ambiguous status, it is up to them to determine whether engaging in communication about racism is likely to lead to their further and greater racial oppression. When, in their determination, this is the case, their political obligation to have these kinds of conversations is defeated or eclipsed. Again, they may still choose to do so; but they are not criticizable if they leave it for another day and another race-based incident.

Sitting With Discomfort

So far, we have focused on the dialogic constraints that hold on those who we might regard as the conversational "leaders" or "initiators." An analysis of the communicative context leads us to conclude that these conversational leaders or initiators ought to take up and deploy our expanded semantics of racism, with its explicit epistemic focus, in conversations that are more akin to call ins than call outs. At the same time, their interlocutors are also subject to dialogic constraints. They must strive to lower their—often instinctive—defenses in order to hear and understand what is being said to them and participate actively in the conversation. When Brianna (Black) tells Jen (white) that she is not being culturally inclusive because she doesn't mention or celebrate Juneteenth at the summer camp she helps direct, Jen has a communicative obligation to engage with Brianna productively rather than take up a number of defensive communicative strategies—such as making a joke, going on the attack, bemoaning her own horribleness in a way that encourages Brianna to soothe her, crying, denying the problem, or going into full-on defense lawyer–mode—all of which would change the subject away from the incident in question. As philosopher Megan Mitchell puts it, "white people have to stop being so damn fragile!"[16] Mitchell understands this requirement to engage in good faith as a moral, political, and epistemological obligation; we include that it is a dialogic constraint as well.

In order to have the kinds of conversations about racism that are necessary to move the United States toward Du Boisian democracy and justice more broadly construed, the interlocutors in these conversations about race-based incidents must communicatively participate, and seek understanding rather than comfort and safety. Here, it is helpful to distinguish between two types of conversations: discussions and arguments. Often, the goal of arguing is to win, whereas the goal of discussion is to come to a resolution that is closer to the heart of the matter. Discussions make progress toward truth; arguments can do this, but do not have to be so aimed. To succeed in an argument, it is enough that you are acknowledged the winner—truth needn't come into play. By contrast, discussions are successful not when one person or side wins, but when those involved acknowledge together that greater understanding has been reached.[17] Oluo writes directly to interlocutors in conversations about race-based incidents that they must always ask themselves, "Am I trying to be right, or am I trying to do better?"[18] Given the purpose of these conversations, interlocutors must work to enter and stay in the conversation as a discussion partner who is trying to be and do better, rather than as an arguer or polemicist. Jen should not debate the merits of declaring Juneteenth a federal holiday in response to Brianna's call in; rather, she should discuss with Brianna how to acknowledge Juneteenth at a US summer camp in a way that is culturally inclusive and apt. As we said above, conversations are a two-way street. The interlocutor must key into having a productive dialogue instead of engaging in argumentation for the sake of winning.

These discussions are not likely to be comfortable: that's ok. As Oluo writes about having this kind of conversation with her mother, "as uncomfortable as this conversation was, it needed to happen . . . we ended the conversation exhausted and emotional, but with a greater understanding of each other."[19] The goal of the interlocutor should be a willingness to sit with their discomfort in order to keep the conversation going as a discussion aimed at greater understanding. This obligation to sit with their discomfort will be helped, we think, by the introduction of our expanded semantics of racism. The new terms we introduce have content—they are not just empty signifiers (that is, new words that have either no meaning or the same meaning as an already-existent term). Telling someone that they have been racially insensitive is not the same as telling them that they are racist! The language we engineer in the following chapter is explicitly epistemically focused, aimed at steering people away from guilt and shame and toward accountability, understanding, and a willingness to change and hold others accountable as well. So, while these necessary conversations about particular race-based incidents and structural racism are likely to be uncomfortable regardless, introducing a new semantics of racism that moves away from the false trinary of racist/not racist/antiracist makes it more likely that interlocuters will be able to meet the dialogic constraints that apply to them.

A CONTINUUM OF PROGRESS

Even when the conversational initiators or leaders meet their dialogic constraints, and their interlocutors meet their dialogic constraints in turn, there is no guarantee of immediate change for the better. What happens after the conversation is dependent, once again, on the capacities of the audience as well as the overall social context. Sometimes, people need to hear something multiple times and via multiple modalities before they are motivated to act; other times, they jump into coordinating with others to transform unjust social processes and practices on the basis of one meaningful conversation. Regardless, the right kinds of conversations are those that are not shut down right off the bat—hence, our argument for particular dialogic constraints on these necessary conversations about the dynamic disaster of racism in the United States. So long as you can keep the conversation going, that is politically and pragmatically better than having someone shut down and walk away or refuse to engage in the first place.

The purpose, recall, is to motivate people to organize collectively towards justice. This is a social process that depends on them changing their minds and coming to believe that a) the United States is unjust and b) that they have a political responsibility to work with others to fix that injustice. This is why the types of conversations we are talking about are so critical—they put people in a place where they are able to change their minds without being coerced. In the classic liberal sense of the term, conversations such as these are *reasonable*, in that they attempt to persuade people by providing good (intellectually respectable) reasons for them to form new beliefs. And it is the rational formation of new beliefs that is likely, we think, to lead people to take up their political responsibility over time. In other words, when people rationally assent to new beliefs, they are more likely to stick with, and follow through on, the implications of those beliefs. (Such as the political obligation to collectively organize to transform oppressive and dominating social processes and practices.) This follows St. Anselm of Canterbury, who noted in the eleventh century that only non-coercive arguments can convince people to change their minds.[20] Coercion can cause people to act *as though* they believe something, but it cannot make them actually believe that thing.[21] For example, threatening someone with a sword and commanding them to assent to Christianity (as happened during the Crusades) is a good way to get someone to act as though they have converted to Christianity; but it cannot really convince them to accept, in their hearts and minds, Christian beliefs. As soon as the person with the sword leaves, they'll go right back to their previous belief system and accompanying actions.

This analysis may help to explain why we are seeing a resurgence of interpersonal race-based incidents in the contemporary United States. You might think that white Americans did not really change their views about Black Americans after the US Civil Rights era of the 1950s and 1960s; they simply learned to be quiet about those views because of economic, social, and political threats. For example, federal laws banning formal discrimination in the workplace were passed, those who openly espoused racist beliefs were socially ostracized, engaging in openly racist politics became a sure way to lose a federal election (although local elections were a different story altogether), and Martin Luther King Jr. was posthumously transformed from the most hated man in America into an American hero.[22] But with the rise of Trump and his ilk, it became more acceptable, and even encouraged, to be racially insensitive, to say racially problematic things and engage in racially troubling behavior. And with this acceptance and encouragement came the resurgence, indicating that the mid-to-late-twentieth-century coercion didn't really work. Many white Americans maintained their racist belief systems and passed them on to the next generation; they simply acted, for a long time, *as though* their minds had been changed.

One response to this resurgence from current racial justice activists has been to physically, socially, or politically threaten those who engage in racially troubling behaviors and so coerce them, as well as other onlookers, into more antiracist behaviors. These tactics and overall goal can be summed up by their slogan, "Make racists afraid again."[23] While there is something to be said for such coercive tactics, they are perhaps unlikely to galvanize those targeted to engage in collective, productive action for democracy and justice over time. For this kind of everyday, long-term activism to occur, people's hearts and minds must be changed. And such change is more often a product of dialogically constrained communication rather than Molotov cocktails.[24]

Of course, these conversations about American racism are not likely to lead to perfection right away. We should instead look for a continuum of progress.[25] The question is not whether people have exactly the correct attitudes and accompanying behaviors, but whether they get better over time. We want people to move from being actively racially insensitive to being passive, and from being passively racially insensitive to being well-intentioned but clueless, and from being well-intentioned but clueless to being allies, and so forth and so on. The semantic route, although it is not the only way, is one way to get people to shift along this continuum.[26] This is true partially because the kinds of conversations that we have described—as opposed to threats and coercion—treat interlocutors as reasonable agents who want to be ethical and just, as "fellow traveler[s]" on a journey of self-reflection and growth that all of us must undertake to some extent if we are to achieve our, and our society's, liberatory potential.[27]

In a letter to his nephew, James Baldwin writes that "We, with love, shall force our brothers to see themselves as they are, to cease fleeing from reality and begin to change it."[28] In his analysis of this passage, philosopher Barrett Emerick argues that Baldwin's notion of love is radical, inclusive, and essential to the fight against oppression. Emerick concludes that Baldwin is calling on us to "stand in moral solidarity" with those that we love, that is, the fellow members of our society with whom we are in community, and "press them to become better while simultaneously understanding that such moral growth is usually a slow and painful process—often, the project of a lifetime."[29] The "forcing" that Baldwin is talking about, then, is not coercive, but a kind of persuasion. To stand with someone as they slowly come to see, with your help, that they've been acting as an agent of oppression and domination, and to help them shift their attitudes and actions in response, is to work with them rather than simply make them afraid. As philosopher George Yancy writes, he "would rather . . . 'good whites' *tarry* with [their] racism and come to terms with how [they] are complicit with more complex interpersonal and institutional forms of white supremacy."[30] To bring about this tarrying, though, this willingness to sit in discomfort and come to new and necessary recognitions, we must, when we are able to do so, be willing to talk with others (our fellow members of society) in a way that helps them move along the continuum of progress. Treating others thusly—with radical love—is difficult, but it is part of how we together begin and continue the hard, and essential, work of changing our reality.[31]

WHAT'S IN IT FOR YOU

If enough people move far enough along the continuum of progress described above, then the contemporary United States will transform into a society where justice is more equally enjoyed by all. This is one key political reason for taking up the semantic shift and expansion that we recommend, and for engaging in the right (a.k.a., dialogically constrained) kinds of conversations about race-based interpersonal incidents and the dynamic disaster of racism in the United States more broadly. If we can get white Americans to tarry with (to use Yancy's language) the unjust background conditions in which they live, and how their attitudes and actions contribute to those oppressive and dominating social processes and practices, in a way that is personally and politically motivating rather than demoralizing, then we have a shot at transforming the United States into a more democratic, more just society. We thus put forth the semantic and communicative route as one (but not the only!) way of getting predominantly white Americans to do this work.

In addition to this political motivation for taking up our proposed semantics and dialogic constraints, which we have discussed at length in this and the previous chapters, there are also interpersonal benefits to be had. Longer, more in-depth communication is likely to strengthen interpersonal bonds, which in turn strengthen both local communities and translocal activist spaces. As social theorists and activists Heidi R. Lewis, Dana Maria Asbury, and Jazlyn Andrews discuss in their volume focused on the experiences of women of color educators, artists, activists, scholars, and other "friends in the struggle," conversations are necessary to address "the always advantageous but sometimes contentious contours of solidarity."[32] When people who are either passively or actively engaging in resistance against oppression have seemingly contradictory goals, it is essential that they communicate rather than shut each other out. That is how you create a community that can survive serious disagreements and that is positioned to support its members when things don't go perfectly (as they inevitably don't). Lewis, Asbury, and Andrews write that this move to interpersonal connection and community- and movement-building through communication honors the Black radical tradition, as exemplified by Du Bois's and Brooker T. Washington's lifelong debate and philosopher, feminist, and activist Audre Lorde's call to create "new patterns of relating across difference."[33] Lorde concludes that it is these relations, if we can make them, that will "mean new paths to our survival."[34]

Bluntly, for our lives to go well, or to continue at all for that matter, we need to be able to lean on each other. And this leaning on, this ability to rely on others, can only occur when we have a way to talk with them about our thoughts, concerns, triumphs, failures, and next steps. We must be able to forge interpersonal relationships, and by extension communities, that can survive racial missteps. Otherwise, we will not survive long. Lorde argues that isolation is the enemy. "We have chosen each other," she writes, and if we do not recognize in "each others battles" that "the war is the same," then our "blood will congeal / upon a dead planet."[35] But if we can meaningfully relate to each other across our differences, "if we win / there is no telling" how far we will rise together.[36] Our proposed semantic shift and dialogic constraints, modest though they are, together give us one more mechanism for creating the interpersonal bonds necessary for us to not only survive, but also flourish.

Finally, it is worth pointing out that language frames and contextualizes our own experiences, as well. As Robin DiAngelo puts it, "language is not neutral . . . the terms and phrases we use shape how we *perceive* or make meaning of what we observe."[37] By expanding our language, we expand our abilities to understand and make sense of ourselves and our world. For example, take the recent introduction of "bisexual" into mainstream conversations about possible sexual and romantic orientations. For many, this term provided a way for them to understand themselves and their desires, as well as others and their desires. What was previously somewhat opaque and difficult to explain, even in their own minds, became perceptible and clear. New language can help create new territories on our mental conceptual maps, or at least sharpen their borders. This in turn can help us to see and make peace with various aspects of our own identities, both in isolation and in relation to our social worlds. To put it bluntly, without self-knowledge, life is likely to be difficult in lots of ways, both internally and externally. So, one reason to expand your semantics, and engage in these kinds of conversations, is to help yourself, to make meaning for yourself in this complicated, messy, rich, and beautiful world.

NOTES

1. From *So You Want to Talk About Race* by Ijeoma Oluo, copyright © 2018. Reprinted by permission of Seal Press, an imprint of Hachette Book Group, Inc.

2. Ijeoma Oluo, *So You Want to Talk about Race*, First ed. (New York: Seal Press, 2018), ch 1, n.p.

3. Beverly Daniel Tatum, *Why are all the Black Kids Sitting Together in the Cafeteria? and Other Conversations about Race* (New York: Perseus Books, 1997), 126.

4. Nikole Hannah-Jones, *The 1619 Project* (New York: New York Times, 2019).

5. *1776 Commission Takes Historic and Scholarly Step to Restore Understanding of the Greatness of the American Founding* (The White House: Washington, D.C., 2021).

6. Kimberley Brownlee, *Conscience and Conviction: The Case for Civil Disobedience* (Oxford: Oxford University Press, 2012), 44.

7. As Robin DiAngelo discusses, this is the difference between being thoughtful and being careful. We must be thoughtful in how we communicate with others about race-based incidents; but we need not be careful, in the sense of avoiding topics for fear of saying the wrong thing or being accused of impoliteness. Robin DiAngelo, *Nice Racism: How Progressive White People Perpetuate Racial Harm* (Boston, MA: Beacon Press, 2021), 103.

8. Upton Sinclair, *I, Candidate for Governor: And how I Got Licked* (Berkeley: University of California Press, 1934), 109.

9. Crystal Bedley, "Engaging Stakeholders on the DEI Journey," *Diverse: Issues in Higher Education,* October 29, 2021.

10. Bedley, "Engaging Stakeholders on the DEI Journey."

11. Bedley, "Engaging Stakeholders on the DEI Journey."

12. James Baldwin, "On being 'White' . . . and Other Lies," in *Black on White: Black Writers on what it Means to be White*, ed. David R. Roediger (New York: Schocken Books, 1998), 180.

13. Du Bois, W. E. B., *Darkwater: Voices from within the Veil* (Champaign, IL: Project Gutenberg, 2005), ch. 2, n.p.

14. Combahee River Collective, "The Combahee River Collective Statement," in *How we Get Free: Black Feminism and the Combahee River Collective*, ed. Keeanga-Yamahtta Taylor (Chicago: Haymarket Books, 2017), 27.

15. For more about complexities of racial ambiguity and mixed race identities (which sometimes do, and sometimes don't, track skin color), see Naomi Zack's work. Comedy also adds another layer of intersectional complexity here; for more on this, see Luvell Anderson's work.

16. Megan Mitchell, "'White People, We Need to Stop being so Damn Fragile!': White and Male Fragility as Epistemic Arrogance," in *Pacifism, Politics, and Feminism: Intersections and Innovations*, ed. Jennifer Kling (Netherlands: Brill Rodopi, 2019), 51–67.

17. Leland Harper, ed., *The Crisis of American Democracy: Essays on a Failing Institution* (Wilmington, DE: Vernon Press, 2022).

18. Oluo, *So You Want to Talk about Race*, ch 3, n.p.

19. Oluo, *So You Want to Talk about Race*, ch 3, n.p.

20. Anselm, "Monologion," in *Anselm of Canterbury: The Major Works*, trans. Brian Davies and G. R. Evans (Oxford: Oxford University Press, 1998).

21. This is one of the major underlying themes of the Netflix series *Hellbound*.

22. Jeanne Theoharis, *A More Beautiful and Terrible History: The Uses and Misuses of Civil Rights History* (Boston, MA: Beacon Press, 2018), ch 6, n.p.

23. Patrick Strickland, "US Anti-Fascists: 'We can make Racists Afraid again,'" *Al Jazeera,* February 21, 2017.

24. We do not rule out the use of coercion and threats altogether to help people overcome the oppressive ideologies to which they are subject and by which they are often infected. Our point is not pacifist in nature, but political and pragmatic. The semantic route is not the only way to create social and political change; but it is the way we are focused on in this book. We discuss other routes elsewhere: see Leland Harper, ed., *The Crisis of American Democracy: Essays on a Failing Institution* (Wilmington, DE: Vernon Press, 2022); Jennifer Kling and Megan Mitchell, *The Philosophy of Protest: Fighting for Justice without Going to War* (Lanham, MD: Rowman & Littlefield International, 2021).

25. This idea is also advocated for by DEI specialist Jennifer Brown. Jennifer Brown, *How to be an Inclusive Leader: Your Role in Creating Cultures of Belonging Where Everyone can Thrive* (New York: Berrett-Koehler Publishers, 2019).

26. Our thanks to Romello Valentine for pushing us to consider the idea of a continuum of progress.

27. Barrett Emerick, "Love and Resistance: Moral Solidarity in the Face of Perceptual Failure," *Feminist Philosophy Quarterly* 2, no. 2 (2016): 16.

28. James Baldwin, *The Fire Next Time* (New York: Vintage Books, 1962), 10.

29. Emerick, "Love and Resistance: Moral Solidarity in the Face of Perceptual Failure," 1.

30. George Yancy, *Black Bodies, White Gazes: The Continuing Significance of Race in America*, Second Edition (New York: Rowman & Littlefield, 2017), 56, emphasis in original.

31. This is exactly what George Yancy does in his NY Times article, "Dear White America," in the editorial blog series The Stone. George Yancy, "Dear White America," *New York Times,* December 24, 2015. He received praise, criticism, and death threats for this article, which prompted him to write the follow-up book *Backlash.* George Yancy, *Backlash: What Happens when we Talk Honestly about Racism in America* (Lanham, MD: Rowman & Littlefield, 2018).

32. Heidi R. Lewis, Dana Maria Asbury and Jazlyn Andrews, *In Audre's Footsteps: Transnational Kitchen Table Talk* (Berlin: edition assemblage, 2021), n.p.

33. Lewis, Asbury and Andrews, *In Audre's Footsteps: Transnational Kitchen Table Talk*; Audre Lorde, "Age, Race, Class, and Sex: Women Redefining Difference," in *Sister Outsider* (Berkeley, CA: Crossing Press, 2007), n.p.

34. Lorde, "Age, Race, Class, and Sex: Women Redefining Difference," n.p.

35. Lorde, "Age, Race, Class, and Sex: Women Redefining Difference," n.p.

36. Lorde, "Age, Race, Class, and Sex: Women Redefining Difference," n.p.

37. DiAngelo, *Nice Racism: How Progressive White People Perpetuate Racial Harm*, xvii, emphasis in original.

Chapter Seven

The Expansion

"Racist" is not—as Richard Spencer argues—a pejorative. It is not the worst word in the English language; it is not the equivalent of a slur. It is descriptive, and the only way to undo racism is to consistently identify and describe it—and then dismantle it. The attempt to turn this usefully descriptive term into an almost unusable slur is, of course, designed to do the opposite: to freeze us into inaction.

—Ibram X. Kendi[1]

The connection between semantics and the dynamic disaster of racism has significant, real-world consequences. Eighteenth-century statesman and abolitionist Frederick Douglass, in his well-known 1890 speech *The Race Problem*,[2] discusses the importance of semantics when it comes to framing public and individual perception. Douglass speaks of the terminology surrounding "the Negro problem," and how it frames Black Americans as the cause of racial disharmony rather than as the ones who are suffering. Douglass argues that the particular language used to frame Black Americans as undesirable and problematic functioned to shape the ensuing narrative. It reinforced the ideas about Blacks held by so many white Southerners, and shifted the ideas about Blacks held by many white Northerners. These ideas then led, unsurprisingly, to actions. Douglass concludes that the connections between semantics, perception, and action are all too real.

Contemporary philosophers Rae Langton, Luvell Anderson, and Sally Haslanger expand on the relationships between race and language, noting that one of the primary functions of language in race is "to attack, spread hatred, [and] create racial hierarchy."[3] After all, language is one of the primary vehicles by which race-based hate is demonstrated and by which race-based harm is caused, or at least initiated. Interpersonally and institutionally, words can and do hurt. So far, we have argued for a shift and expansion in our semantics, to more adequately describe and characterize race-based situations in order to facilitate better and more meaningful dialogue about those situations. Here, we begin the work for which we call.

We argue that *racial insensitivity* is a term that, once defined and applied more broadly, can do significant work in the discourse of racism.[4] The addition of this term to the race-based lexicon helps us to break free from the semantic false trinary of racist/not racist/antiracist and the character evaluations to which it leads. Ridding ourselves of this false trinary allows us to more accurately describe at least some of the race-based situations in which we find ourselves and, in turn, enables us to more accurately perceive, reflect on, and address these situations at both the interpersonal and institutional levels. By turning the focus to insensitivity (which is usually knowledge and awareness-based) rather than accusations of good and evil (which are usually character-based), we contend that more fruitful conversations will take place. As discussed in previous chapters, these conversations are a necessary stepping stone to community building, which is a key component, insofar as it is conducive to democracy and justice, to ending the dynamic disaster of racism in the United States.

THE IMPORTANCE OF LANGUAGE

The relation between language and perception is explored across multiple disciplines and sub-disciplines, including psychology, linguistics, epistemology, philosophy of language, and hermeneutics.[5] Philosophy of race and critical race theory are no different— prominent historical and contemporary thinkers have long explored and addressed the connections between race and language. From Frederick Douglass's words on how language serves as a framing mechanism to the ideas discussed by Rae Langton, Luvell Anderson, and Sally Haslanger about how language is one primary method by which we communicate and demonstrate race-based hatred, language matters; it is not just a throwaway, but integral to our lives and politics. Similarly, Malcolm X describes his experience with language and how his mastery of words, both spoken and written, proved valuable for him before his civil rights pursuits and how a complete revision of the way that he used language was essential for him, not only to be noticed by people of power and the masses but also to move forward in his own personal pursuit of civil rights.[6] Malcolm X was a street hustler and used the vernacular appropriate to that context. But that vernacular was not appropriate to all contexts; when he moved into political advocacy and activism, Malcolm X discovered that it was more effective to revise his language to connect with others in this new context. Today, we might call this code switching.

Drawing perhaps the strongest connections between language and race is social theorist and revolutionary Frantz Fanon, who argues that language is an essential component of social conditioning and the vehicle by which racism is carried through and between societies.[7] Fanon then takes this idea even further, arguing that language can be and has been weaponized by colonizers and oppressors to maintain their positions of power.[8] In the realm of race relations, language, and the particular terminology of which we avail ourselves, serves as a powerful tool in shaping the injustices that we see, in helping us to recognize and process these injustices, and in crafting solutions to remedy these injustices. This is precisely why we focus on the semantic route—while revolution might be necessary, in the end, to transform the United States into a more democratic and just society, how we understand that revolution and its consequences will need to be framed by language.

RACIAL INSENSITIVITY

The best way to start building the argument for *racial insensitivity* is by revisiting a fictional, though possibly familiar, example that was presented in chapter two. We use this example as a reference point for the forthcoming discussion.

> Suppose a young, white family is preparing for a fun-filled Halloween evening. In their preparations, the 6-year-old daughter puts on her costume that her parents purchased for her at a local big-box store; one which depicts (rather poorly) the ceremonial garb of a nondescript indigenous tribe. Upon putting on her costume, her parents promptly send her out with her group of friends and a neighborhood parent to go trick-or-treating.[9]

Let us also add the further specifications that this is a generally lovely and thoughtful family who harbors no ill-will toward any particular race, religion, or ethnicity and that this costume was the only one available that was in the correct size for the daughter and within an affordable price range for the family. What exactly are we to make of this situation? How should we classify it? Applying the false trinary of racist/not racist/antiracist (which we are forced to do, given our current semantic limitations), leaves us unable to fully or accurately consider and communicate about this situation, with either the family themselves or others. This situation isn't easy; imagine trying to describe it to a friend. Would Leland text Jen and tell her about his racist neighbors? Probably not; but at the same time, it's not clearly a non-issue. It warrants discussion of *some* kind (insert confused handwaving here).

We would venture that a significant number of people would have a problem with this situation; that is, they would not see it as benign. A crudely made Pocahontas costume is fundamentally different from a crudely made *Finding Nemo* costume, or a crudely made Jack Sparrow costume—there is a racial undertone to this situation.[10] One needs only to look at the strained history between Indigenous peoples in North America and whites to understand why strong feelings about situations like this exist. This history includes, but is not limited to, theft of land and resources, genocide, residential schools, scapegoating, erasure, marginalization, and cultural appropriation. Given such historical and ongoing oppression, it is easy to interpret the above situation as racist, or at least to grasp why many people would interpret it as problematic.

Alternatively, there are many others who would be reluctant to describe this situation as racist, and who would certainly be reluctant to describe the agents involved so negatively (recall that *racist* in common parlance is heard as an attribution of bad character, regardless of whether its use is so intended).[11] This reluctance might stem from the idea that this situation does not meet or surpass some kind of minimum threshold that is required to deem something *racist*. There are several legitimate reasons that one could hold this position. The first is that neither the parents nor the child were intentionally trying to wrong anybody. Although it is not the whole of the issue, intentions do matter in such race-based cases. We have stipulated that there are no bad intentions in this situation, that we know of, because we think it matches how our interactions in the real world ordinarily go— we often don't know people's intentions, as it is difficult to get people to confess to having intentionally racist plans. (In other words, it's very hard to get people to check the "racist" box on a hiring form.) In the absence of such knowledge, we have to do the best we can with people's actions; hence, the importance of calling them in rather than out, and seeing what they do in response. The parents, some might think, were just trying to help their daughter fit in with her peers, the best way that they could, given the means available to them. Similarly, the daughter was just being a kid who wanted to feel included by taking part in a typically harmless annual childhood tradition with her friends. Many would claim that the parents were simply doing what they thought was best for their child—something that we all strive to do with our children—and that the daughter is too young either to know better or to make different choices. We can see how these thoughts would lead to a reluctance to ascribe either liability for the situation or a negative evaluation of their characters.

From a critical thinking perspective, the temptation here might be to withhold judgment. Groups disagree, and each group has good reasons for its view. However, this is not a situation where we can withhold judgment.[12] We either have to act like something race-based is happening, or like something race-based is not happening. So, we must make a determination: is the situation worthy of communicating with the family in question, or others, about its race-based nature? Or should we let it go as benign, and regard those who view it as racist as being mistaken? We have to make the call—you can't sit on the fence here. Leland either texts Jen about his neighbors and their daughter's costume, or he doesn't.

Our term, *racial insensitivity*, gives us a way to get off the fence without committing ourselves to either writing off the family as racist or dismissing their actions as perfectly acceptable in an ostensibly diverse, inclusive, democratic, just society. Calling the situation racially insensitive acknowledges that something race-based is going on here, and a response is required, without assuming that the family knew better and acted from malice rather than ignorance. It puts them in the category of being epistemically blameworthy rather than being morally blameworthy. Being epistemically at fault, while still not a desirable position to be in, is far better, for most people, than being morally at fault.[13] They are racially insensitive—we can and should criticize them for not even thinking about the fact that their daughter's costume, in the context of their society, is highly likely to be read as a problem. Following Young (see chapter four), regardless of the origins of their ignorance, they are accountable for it—they must try to be more thoughtful about the racial contours and context of their lives and society. Going back to our boat analogy from chapter four, they don't even recognize that we're all sinking. So, to them, it is appropriate to say, "How do you not see this hole? Grab a damn bucket!"

Then, it all depends on their response to being called in as racially insensitive. They may take it well (as we hope will be encouraged by our new term and dialogic constraints) or they may reject being invited to dialogue about these issues. Let us contrast this case with another situation that took place around Halloween 2021 in Kelowna, British Columbia, Canada.[14] A home there was decorated for Halloween with, among other things, a US confederate flag and a dark-skinned figure hanging from a noose. The figure hanging from the noose was life-sized, fully clothed, had what appeared to be stuffed black disposable gloves for hands, and a stuffed black material sack for the head. News of this home and its Halloween decorations quickly spread nationally, featuring interviews from local townspeople, neighbors, local police, the Mayor, and eventually, the owner of the home in question. In a statement, the owner—who chose to remain anonymous—claimed that there was no malicious intent behind those particular decorations, that he had no racial ill-will toward any particular racial group, and that the decorations were put in place simply because he enjoyed the colors in the confederate flag and because the life-sized dark-skinned figure hanging from a noose fit in thematically with the rest of his Halloween decorations.

If we are to interpret the homeowner's actions in the most charitable of lights, we might consider this to be a case of racial insensitivity. But, to continue the story, after having been made aware by the media, the police, local politicians, and local townspeople, that these particular Halloween decorations were harming others, the homeowner still refused to remove either the confederate flag or the life-sized dark-skinned figure hanging from a noose. It is this subsequent refusal that leads us to make the shift from viewing him as racially insensitive to viewing him as racist. The reason for this is that he is now in possession of all of the necessary information—he knows that his decorations are offensive and harmful to Black (and other) members of the community—yet he has chosen to not alter his behavior. In contrast to the fictional example, where the family simply fails to think about the context of their society and their daughter's costume's racial undertones, this guy has been explicitly called in and asked to change his offensive and harmful behavior, and he refused. People have done the work with him, and instead of picking up a bucket (to go back to our sinking boat analogy), he makes the hole in the boat bigger.

We are now equipped to explain the Mitch McConnell case with which we began our Preface. Is he that stupid, or that racist? Answer: Both! It is stupid to not update your beliefs in light of new information, and it is racist to refuse to change your behaviors after you have been called in and people have worked to explain to you the dynamic disaster of racism, your role in its perpetuation, and your possible role in bringing about a more democratic, more just society. Mitch McConnell could organize with others to transform US society, and he has been communicated with *ad nauseum* about this need. We know this because late US senator and US civil rights icon John Lewis said publicly, many times, that he had discussed race and racism with McConnell in hopes of changing his views. It is also essential to remember that McConnell is eighty years old and has been in public service since the mid-1970s—he has had plenty of time to educate himself about the realities of racism in the United States.

Furthermore, McConnell has had, and still has, the opportunity to do this essential transformative work in collaboration with others. In fact, given his position in society (at the time of writing, he is the US Senate Minority Leader, and for several previous years was the US Senate Majority Leader), it is reasonable to conclude that he has a greater-than-usual responsibility to do so. Following our conclusion in chapter four, everyone is responsible for working together to bring about justice. The context of US society though, makes it the case that some people—namely, those in positions of privilege and power—have a greater degree of responsibility, not because they are more liable, but because they are equally accountable and have more power. And yet, McConnell continues to make the kinds of egregious comments that deny reality, and to act in ways that exacerbate the dynamic disaster of racism, rather than working with others to bring any relief.

In some ways, it is easier to focus on the Halloween decorations in Kelowna, Mitch McConnell's public commentary, or Christine Caswell's calling the police on Boston Red Sox Hall-of-Famer Tommy Harper (or any other race-based "Karen" incident, for that matter). These race-based incidents so clearly contribute to, and are part of, the dynamic disaster of racism, that they are easy to categorize within the semantic false trinary of racist/not racist/antiracist. However, focusing exclusively on such cases, as US and global media tend to do, reinforces the false trinary, and so contributes to the false belief that if you're not doing anything analogous to such cases, you're not doing anything wrong. This in turn contributes to white fragility—when people only have the language to categorize situations so extremely, equally extreme responses are provoked. Nuanced conversations about the bulk of race-based incidents, which are not often like those commonly depicted in the media but are more like the cases we see in our everyday lives (some of which we have described in this book), are shut down before they can even start. Thus, white supremacy and the dynamic disaster of racism continues, preventing the transformation of the United States into a Du Boisian democracy where justice is more equally enjoyed by all. As a partial remedy for this complex problem, we introduce the term *racial insensitivity*, which better and more accurately describes the situations that we are more likely to encounter in our day-to-day lives. It provides us with a way to call people in that is not necessarily character-based; the hope is that we can thus avoid triggering their white fragility, and so communicate with them productively, in ways that lead to positive change.

FURTHER CONSIDERATIONS

Having concluded our positive argument, we turn our attention to some remaining questions and concerns. First, you might worry that *racial insensitivity* may only apply to a small portion of the race-based situations that cannot be accurately or adequately captured by the semantic false trinary of racist/not racist/antiracist. *Racial insensitivity* may still leave us lacking sufficient terminology with which to characterize many race-based situations.

Part of the dynamic nature of racism is that it constantly changes; thus, it is likely that new situations will arise that cannot be appropriately captured by the term *racial insensitivity*. We have just scratched the surface of this issue. Still, we think that we have gone some way, in this book, to explaining why more terminology is necessary. While we are only able to introduce one term here, our argument does not preclude the development of additional language with which to describe the multiplicity of race-based incidents and situations. So, we call for more work to determine how *racial insensitivity* may or may not apply to a variety of race-based situations, and for the development of additional terms if necessary (as we think is likely to be the case). We have started this work, but not finished it—like achieving racial justice, ours is a social project. It requires collaboration and fine-tuning from multiple perspectives and voices.

Second, some will not be amenable to this "softening the blow" kind of approach to addressing race-based situations, which works with white fragility rather than trying to push through it. Proponents of this response argue that our kind of approach puts the onus on the individual fighting for justice to make those who fail to see the dynamic disaster of racism more comfortable. They may say that if somebody's feelings are hurt because they got called out for bringing about a racially problematic situation, so be it. Furthermore, calling them out and hurting their feelings may, in fact, provide them with the shock necessary to cause them to think more deeply before acting again in a similar manner. As is evident from the writings of activists such as Martin Luther King Jr., Malcolm X, Nelson Mandela, and others, they think that demanding justice, rather than asking nicely for it, is what works. As Frederick Douglass puts it,

> Power concedes nothing without a demand. It never did and it never will. Find out just what any people will quietly submit to and you have found out the exact measure of injustice and wrong which will be imposed upon them, and these will continue till they are resisted with either words or blows, or with both. The limits of tyrants are prescribed by the endurance of those whom they oppress.[15]

Here, we begin the resistance with words. However, if that doesn't work, we are amenable to the further steps called for by Douglass and others. Our point in this book is simply that we haven't yet been able to really try words, because we have so far lacked sufficient language to have the kinds of conversations called for by W. E. B. Du Bois, Iris Marion Young, George Yancy, and others. Should those dialogically constrained conversations fail to move enough people far enough along the continuum of progress at a reasonable pace, then we are open to other options. Basically, our move is to soft sell first with the new semantic tools provided; then, if needed, move to the hard sell.[16]

Racially insensitive, while it is not the silver bullet to end all racial injustice, is a term that can, in certain instances, promote meaningful dialogue and, hopefully, lead to further social progress.

OTHER TERMS

We have suggested a term that we think could function in the way that we want it to and could alleviate some of the problems that we discuss. But we acknowledge that *racial insensitivity* may not be the correct term and that it may not ever receive widespread uptake in the way that we would need it to. Academics often try to coin new terms to account for various states of affairs in our world in the hope (perhaps naively) that these terms will make it into the everyday language of the masses. Of course, this is simply not how language tends to work—with words and phrases being tossed to the masses from the ivory tower. While it is the case that uptake does not occur in this way, there are still parameters to which any new term must adhere if it is to successfully serve the proper function. As such, we are open to the application of new and different terms, in addition to or in replacement of *racial insensitivity*, to supplement the existing semantic lexicon for race-based situations. However, there is a set of criteria that each proposed addition must satisfy before it can be considered a viable candidate.

To begin, any proposed term has to be functional; it cannot be merely an empty signifier that is the linguistic equivalent of confused handwaving. Consider the following conversation, in response to a complex race-based incident or situation that does not fall neatly into the racist/not racist/antiracist false trinary:

Leland: "Well, that happened."

Jen: "Yeah. That was a thing, alright."

Leland: "It was definitely something."

Jen: "Yeah no for sure—it was a whole thing."

In this conversation, the term *thing* is being used as an empty signifier; it doesn't tell us anything about the nature of the incident in question or give us any indication of how Leland and Jen are characterizing it to each other. Depending purely on their intonation and inflection, Jen and Leland could be confused, aggrieved, disappointed, sad, taken aback, amazed, shocked, etc. They are using *thing* here as a kind of shorthand for the semantic gap that we've been describing throughout the book—it captures not the nature of the situation itself, but rather that they don't quite know how to describe, characterize, or explain that situation. By contrast, *racial insensitivity* is functional, in that it captures something about the nature of the race-based incident or situation at issue, and so gives people a way to characterize it that is both more accurate and meaningful to themselves and others. Any term that is proposed in *racial insensitivity*'s stead, or in addition to it, must be likewise functional.

In addition, for a term to be a viable candidate for our semantic response to the dynamic disaster of racism, it must capture that the agents involved in the race-based situation are epistemically at fault without importing the conclusion that they are necessarily *morally* at fault as well. In other words, the term must not, in the first instance, attack people's characters. The key semantic expansion with which we are concerned is the move away from language that straightforwardly and immediately divides the world into good people and evil people (as the false trinary of racist/not racist/antiracist does), and toward language that criticizes people for their thoughtlessness and holds them accountable, without writing them off altogether, for their failure to take the racial context of their society into consideration before acting. Once we have such language, meeting the dialogic constraints that we set out in chapter six becomes easier, and so the right kinds of conversations are more likely to occur. We think *racial insensitivity* fulfills this role nicely; it captures a lack of awareness and care without writing anyone off morally as a lost cause right off the bat, and so allows for call ins rather than call outs. (Writing them off may come later, of course, depending on the person's response to being called in as racially insensitive; see our discussion above.) To be workable, any term proposed must involve this same kind of semantic shift.

Related to this shift from the moral to the epistemic is the criterion that the term needs to have a better chance than *racist* of not triggering white fragility. Recall that the goal of the semantic route is to call people into conversations, to help them tarry with their role in upholding racial injustice and oppression and become motivated to work together with others to transform American society. These conversations cannot occur when white fragility is triggered, as it so often is when the term *racist* is used. To be sure, white fragility is a tricky beast; there is no guarantee that *racially insensitive*, or any other similar term that meets the criteria we set out, will not trigger it as well. But we think that the shift toward the epistemic makes such a term less likely to trigger white fragility, and thus useful in garnering appropriate interpersonal and institutional responses to the dynamic disaster of racism. Regardless, any term that is less likely than *racist* to trigger white fragility may be acceptable (assuming that it meets the other criteria as well).

Finally, any proposed term needs to have a reasonable chance of widespread social uptake. Getting people and institutions to respond appropriately to the dynamic disaster that is racism in the United States is a social and political project. If other people cannot understand you when you attempt to call them in to have the conversations that might lead them to conclude that a strong institutional and interpersonal response is demanded, then there is no chance of such a response occurring. Creating conversational spaces where we actually talk to each other rather than past each other about race-based situations, and racism in the United States more broadly, requires some shared terminology, which in turn requires widespread (if not universal) uptake. Again, we think *racially insensitive* has a chance here, in part because discussions about sensitivity, or a lack thereof, are already part of American popular culture. Adding the modifier "racially," to make clear what the charge of insensitivity is in reference to, doesn't seem like too much of a stretch. But we could be wrong about this; that's fine. Any term that gains widespread uptake, and meets the other three criteria as well, could supplement the semantics surrounding racism in the United States in exactly the right kind of way.

Historically, new terms that gain widespread uptake arise organically in subcultural spaces and then spread outwards to the society as a whole. A classic example of this is the American LGBTQ+ community, which initially created, adapted, and adopted many of the terms that are now commonly used throughout the United States to discuss gender and sexuality. "Bisexual," which we discussed in chapter six, is a case in point, as is the now-widespread use of the gender-neutral word "partner" in place of the more traditional "husband" or "wife" to describe someone's long-term significant other. These terms were initially niche, but gradually gained broad acceptance with the social and political changes that have occurred in the last fifty or so years. Activist spaces also often deliberately create new language and vocabulary to re-frame and re-conceptualize the issues at stake. As Serbian political activist Srdja Popovic writes, if you can get the public to frame and discuss the issues using the language that the activists put forth, that is half the battle right there.[17] Think here about the phrase "the one percent"; before the Occupy Movement, no one—outside of some economists and activists—knew what that meant. Now, we use it in casual conversation all the time, and it has arguably made the bulk of American society more aware of, and sensitive to, large-scale economic inequality. The general acceptance of the term "the one percent" has provided us with a way to understand and talk about such inequality, which may yet lead to economic changes at all levels. (We can hope.)

So, for those who do not quite like *racial insensitivity* as a term, we encourage looking to subcultural and activist spaces for new and different terminology that might fit the criteria we set out. Our project is social; we call for a semantic shift in order to, ultimately, motivate people to work together to bring about democracy and justice more equally enjoyed by all. It would go against the grain to insist that our proposed term alone is apt for that purpose. We welcome a greater semantic expansion that will enable us to more accurately describe, discuss, and respond to race-based incidents and situations. We have begun that expansion here—after arguing for why it is necessary and important for most of the book—and hope others will join us in this work. We must address the insufficiency in our language to have a hope of addressing, and relieving, the dynamic disaster of American antiBlack racism.

NOTES

1. Excerpt from *HOW TO BE AN ANTIRACIST* by Ibram X. Kendi, copyright © 2019 by Ibram X. Kendi. Used by permission of One World, an imprint of Random House, a division of Penguin Random House LLC. All rights reserved.

2. Frederick Douglass, *The Race Problem* (Washington, DC: Great speech of Frederick Douglass, delivered before the Bethel Literary and Historical Association, in the Metropolitan A.M.E. Church, 1890).

3. Rae Langton, Luvell Anderson and Sally Haslanger, "Language and Race," in *Routledge Companion to the Philosophy of Language*, eds. Gillian Russell and Delia Graff Fara (New York: Routledge, 2012), 753.

4. We thank an anonymous reviewer for pointing out the fact that people already employ the term *racial insensitivity* to categorize certain situations. Our argument, however, is that *racial insensitivity* ought to be defined more precisely in the literature, utilized more frequently in our everyday use as an alternative to other terminology that is already in place, and that it can be used to fill an important explanatory gap.

5. For those interested in pursuing research which draws connections between language, perception, and cognition see, among others, Noam Chomsky, *Reflections on Language* (New York: Pantheon, 1975); Ray Jackendoff, *Semantics and Cognition* (Cambridge: MIT Press, 1983); Daniel Casasanto et al., "How Deep are Effects of Language on Thought?: Time Estimation in Speakers of English, Indonesian, Greek, and Spanish," in *Proceedings of the 26th Annual Cognitive Science Society*, eds. Kenneth Forbus, Dedre Gentner and Terry Regier (Mahwah: Lawrence Erlbaum Associates Inc., 2004), 186–91; Lera Boroditsky, "How Language Shapes Thought: The Languages we Speak Affect our Perceptions of the World," *Scientific American*, February 2011; Guy Deutscher, *Through the Language Glass: Why the World Looks Different in Other Languages* (New York: Arrow Books, 2011); Catherine L. Caldwell-Harris, "Our Language Affects what we See: A New Look at the 'Russian Blues' Demonstrates the Power of Words to Shape Perception," *Scientific American*, January 15, 2019.

6. Malcolm X and Alex Haley, *The Autobiography of Malcolm X: As Told to Alex Haley* (New York: Ballantine Books, 1992), 195–219.

7. Frantz Fanon, *Black Skin, White Masks* (New York: Grove Press, 1967).

8. Frantz Fanon, *The Wretched of the Earth* (New York: Grove Press, 1963), 7.

9. Page 17.

10. As well as cultural and ethnic undertones.

11. For more on how the term *racist* is heard, see chapters two and six.

12. The necessity of making a decision about what is true because it has real-world consequences is sometimes called practical or pragmatic encroachment. Brian Kim and Matthew McGrath, eds., *Pragmatic Encroachment in Epistemology* (New York: Routledge, 2019).

13. Of course, this is not true for everyone; however, we think it is the case for the vast bulk of Americans. See chapter six for more on this claim.

14. Shelby Thom and Darrian Matassa-Fung, "'Disgusting' Halloween Display Featuring Confederate Flag and Noose Haunts Kelowna Resident," *Global News,* October 27, 2021.

15. Frederick Douglass, *West India Emancipation* (New York: speech delivered at Canandaigua, New York, on the twenty-third anniversary of the West India Emancipation, 1857).

16. Importantly, this isn't respectability politics. We're not calling on any group to act more like the dominant group in order to gain power; rather, we are calling on those in a position to do so to have thoughtful, nuanced conversations about racism that focus on holding people accountable and motivating them to work in concert with others to change themselves and their society.

17. Srdja Popovic, *Blueprint for Revolution: How to use Rice Pudding, Lego Men, and Other Nonviolent Techniques to Galvanize Communities, Overthrow Dictators, Or Simply Change the World* (New York: Spiegel & Grau, 2015), ch. 8.

Bibliography

ACLED. *A Year of Racial Justice Protests: Key Trends in Demonstrations Support-ing the BLM Movement.* The Armed Conflict Location & Event Data Project, 2021.

"African American Health: Creating Equal Opportunities for Health." *Centers for Disease Control and Prevention,* July 3, 2017. https://www.cdc.gov/vitalsigns/aahealth/index.html.

Alexander, Michelle. "The New Jim Crow." *Ohio State Journal of Criminal Law* 9, no. 1 (2011): 7–26.

———. *The New Jim Crow: Mass Incarceration in the Age of Colorblindness.* New York: The New Press, 2012.

Anderson, Carol. *White Rage: The Unspoken Truth of our Racial Divide.* New York: Bloomsbury USA, an imprint of Bloomsbury Publishing Plc, 2016.

Anselm. "Monologion." In *Anselm of Canterbury: The Major Works.* Translated by Davies, Brian and G. R. Evans. Oxford: Oxford University Press, 1998.

Baldwin, James. *The Fire Next Time.* New York: Vintage Books, 1962.

———. "On being 'White'. . . and Other Lies." In *Black on White: Black Writers on what it Means to be White*, edited by Roediger, David R., 177–80. New York: Schocken Books, 1998.

Basevich, Elvira. "W. E. B. Du Bois's Critique of American Democracy during the Jim Crow Era: On the Limitations of Rawls and Honneth." *The Journal of Political Philosophy* 27, no. 3 (2019): 318–40.

Bauder, David. "AP Says it Will Capitalize Black but Not White." *AP News,* July 20, 2020. https://apnews.com/article/entertainment-cultures-race-and-ethnicity-us-news-ap-top-news-7e36c00c5af0436abc09e051261fff1f.

Bedley, Crystal. "Engaging Stakeholders on the DEI Journey." *Diverse: Issues in Higher Education,* October 29, 2021. https://www.diverseeducation.com/opinion/article/15280707/dei.

Begnaud, David. "How Citizens Turned into Saviors After Katrina Struck." *CBS News,* August 29, 2015. https://www.cbsnews.com/news/remembering-the-cajun-navy-10-years-after-hurricane-katrina/.

Bloch, Arthur. *Murphy's Law Book Two: More Reasons Why Things Go Wrong!* Los Angeles: Price Stern Sloan, 1980.

Blum, Lawrence. "Varieties of Racial Ills." In *"I'm Not a Racist, but . . .": The Moral Quandary of Race*, 53–77. New York: Cornell University Press, 2002.

Boroditsky, Lera. "How Language Shapes Thought: The Languages we Speak Affect our Perceptions of the World." *Scientific American*, February 2011.

Bourdieu, Pierre. *The Field of Cultural Production: Essays on Art and Literature*, edited by Johnson, Randal. New York: Columbia University Press, 1993.

Brown, Jennifer. *How to be an Inclusive Leader: Your Role in Creating Cultures of Belonging Where Everyone Can Thrive.* New York: Berrett-Koehler Publishers, 2019.

Brownlee, Kimberley. *Conscience and Conviction: The Case for Civil Disobedience.* Oxford: Oxford University Press, 2012.

Cahill, Ann J. "Unjust Sex Vs Rape." *Hypatia* 31, no. 4 (2016): 746–61.

Caldwell-Harris, Catherine L. "Our Language Affects what we See: A New Look at the 'Russian Blues' Demonstrates the Power of Words to Shape Perception." *Scientific American*, January 15, 2019.

Casasanto, Daniel, Lera Boroditsky, Webb Phillips, Jesse Greene, Shima Goswami, Simon Bocanegra-Thiel, Ilia Santiago-Diaz, Olga Fotokopoulu, Ria Pita, and David Gil. "How Deep are Effects of Language on Thought?: Time Estimation in Speakers of English, Indonesian, Greek, and Spanish." In *Proceedings of the 26th Annual Cognitive Science Society*, edited by Forbus, Kenneth, Dedre Gentner and Terry Regier, 186–91. Mahwah: Lawrence Erlbaum Associates Inc., 2004.

Chomsky, Noam. *Reflections on Language.* New York: Pantheon, 1975.

Christiano, Thomas, ed. *Philosophy and Democracy: An Anthology.* Oxford: Oxford University Press, 2003.

———. *The Rule of the Many: Fundamental Issues in Democratic Theory.* Boulder, CO: Westview Press, 1996.

Christiano, Tom and Sameer Bajaj. "Democracy." *The Stanford Encyclopedia of Philosophy*, Fall 2021.

Ciaramella, C. J. "8 of the Top 10 Biggest U.S. Coronavirus Hotspots are Prisons and Jails." *Reason,* April 29, 2020. https://reason.com/2020/04/29/8-of-the-top-10-biggest-u-s-coronavirus-hotspots-are-prisons-and-jails/.

Colangelo, Sara (dir.). *Worth.* MadRiver Pictures. Netflix. 2020.

Combahee River Collective. "The Combahee River Collective Statement." In *How we Get Free: Black Feminism and the Combahee River Collective*, edited by Taylor, Keeanga-Yamahtta, 15–27. Chicago: Haymarket Books, 2017.

Cooper, Brittney. *Eloquent Rage.* New York: St. Martins Press, 2018.

"Coronavirus in the U.S.: Latest Map and Case Count." *New York Times,* updated May 3, 2020. https://www.nytimes.com/interactive/2020/us/coronavirus-us-cases.html.

Cukier, Kenneth, Viktor Mayer-Schönberger, and Francis de Véricourt. *Framers: Human Advantage in an Age of Technology and Turmoil.* New York: Dutton, 2021.

Dahl, Robert A. *Democracy and its Critics.* New Haven: Yale University Press, 1991.

Darby, Derrick and John L. Rury. *The Color of Mind: Why the Origins of the Achieve-ment Gap Matter for Justice.* Illinois: University of Chicago Press, 2018. https://press.uchicago.edu/ucp/books/book/chicago/C/bo27527445.html.

Deutscher, Guy. *Through the Language Glass: Why the World Looks Different in Other Languages.* New York: Arrow Books, 2011.

DiAngelo, Robin. *Nice Racism: How Progressive White People Perpetuate Racial Harm.* Boston, Massachusetts: Beacon Press, 2021.

———. *White Fragility: Why It's so Hard for White People to Talk about Racism.* Boston: Beacon Press Books, 2018.

Ditter, Bob. *To Tell the Truth.* California: Healthy Learning, 2013.

Douglass, Frederick. *The Race Problem.* Washington, D.C.: Great speech of Freder-ick Douglass, delivered before the Bethel Literary and Historical Association, in the Metropolitan A.M.E. Church, 1890.

———. *West India Emancipation.* New York: speech delivered at Canandaigua, New York, on the twenty-third anniversary of the West India Emancipation, 1857.

Du Bois, W. E. B. *Black Reconstruction.* New York: Free Press, 1992.

———. *Darkwater: Voices from within the Veil.* Champaign, Ill: Project Gutenberg, 2005.

———. "The Immediate Problem of the American Negro." *The Crisis* 9, no. 6 (1915): n.p. https://blackfreedom.proquest.com/the-immediate-problem-of-the -american-negro/.

———. *The Souls of Black Folk.* New York: Taylor & Francis, 2004.

Editors of Encyclopaedia Britannica. "Hurricane Katrina." *Encyclopedia Britannica,* September 8, 2021. https://www.britannica.com/event/Hurricane-Katrina.

Emerick, Barrett. "Love and Resistance: Moral Solidarity in the Face of Perceptual Failure." *Feminist Philosophy Quarterly* 2, no. 2 (2016): 1–21.

Fanon, Frantz. *Black Skin, White Masks.* New York: Grove Press, 1967.

———. *The Wretched of the Earth.* New York: Grove Press, 1963.

Feinberg, Joel. "Collective Responsibility." *Journal of Philosophy* 65, no. 21 (1968): 674–88.

French, Peter, ed. *Individual and Collective Responsibility.* Rochester, VT: Schenk-man, 1998.

Fricker, Miranda. *Epistemic Injustice: Power and the Ethics of Knowing.* Oxford: Oxford University Press, 2007.

Frye, Marilyn. "Oppression." In *The Politics of Reality*, 1–16. New York: Crossing Press, 1983.

Garcia, J. L. A. "The Heart of Racism." *Journal of Social Philosophy* 27, no. 1 (1996): 5–45.

Gavey, Nicola. *Just Sex?: The Cultural Scaffolding of Rape.* New York: Routledge, 2005.

Glaude Jr., Eddie S. *Democracy in Black: How Race Still Enslaves the American Soul.* New York: Broadway Books, 2017.

Hafiz. "Covers Her Face with Both Hands." *The Gift: Poems by Hafiz, the Great Sufi Master*, translated by Daniel Ladinsky. New York: Penguin Books, 1999.

Handelsman, Walt. "Our Views: Cajun Navy Rescues our Sense of Spirit." *The Advocate,* September 24, 2016. https://www.theadvocate.com/baton_rouge/opinion/our_views/article_3f08736e-8037-11e6-986e-a77c965f39f2.html.

Hannah-Jones, Nikole. *The 1619 Project.* New York: New York Times, 2019.

Hansen, Claire. "116th Congress by Party, Race, Gender, and Religion." *U.S. News & World Report,* January 3, 2019.

Harper, Leland, ed. *The Crisis of American Democracy: Essays on a Failing Institution.* Wilmington, DE: Vernon Press, 2022.

Harper, Leland. "Fear and the Importance of Race-Based Data in COVID-19 Policy Implementation." *Global Discourse: An Interdisciplinary Journal of Current Affairs* 11, no. 3 (2021): 433–39.

Haslanger, Sally. "What is a Social Practice?" *Royal Institute of Philosophy Supplement* 82, (2018): 231–47. doi:10.1017/s1358246118000085.

Hooker, Juliet. "Black Lives Matter and the Paradoxes of U.S. Black Politics: From Democratic Sacrifice to Democratic Repair." *Political Theory* 44, no. 4 (2016): 448–69. doi:10.1177/0090591716640314.

Hutchinson, Bill. "From 'BBQ Becky' to 'Golfcart Gail,' List of Unnecessary 911 Calls made on Blacks Continues to Grow." *ABC News,* October 19, 2018. https://abcnews.go.com/US/bbq-becky-golfcart-gail-list-unnecessary-911-calls/story?id=58584961.

Jackendoff, Ray. *Semantics and Cognition.* Cambridge: MIT Press, 1983.

Jones, Stacy. "White Men Account for 72% of Corporate Leadership at 16 Fortune 500 Companies." *Fortune,* June 9, 2017.

Kendi, Ibram X. *How to be an Antiracist.* First ed. New York: One World, 2019.

Kim, Brian and Matthew McGrath, eds. *Pragmatic Encroachment in Epistemology.* New York: Routledge, 2019.

King Jr., Martin Luther. "A Letter from Birmingham Jail." *The Atlantic Monthly* 212.2, August 1963.

Kling, Jennifer and Leland Harper. "The Semantic Foundations of White Fragility and the Consequences for Justice." *Res Philosophica* 97, no. 2 (2020): 325–44. doi:10.11612/resphil.1891.

Kling, Jennifer and Megan Mitchell. *The Philosophy of Protest: Fighting for Justice without Going to War.* Lanham, MD: Rowman & Littlefield International, 2021.

Kobal, Jan (dir.) "This Pandemic." *Coronavirus, Explained.* Netflix. 2020.

Kruesi, Kimberlee and Jonathan Mattise. "Tennessee Gov Signs Bill Upping Penalties on some Protests." *AP News,* August 21, 2020. https://apnews.com/f465062c6eb6ab38c8df99b40f687fe4.

Langton, Rae, Luvell Anderson, and Sally Haslanger. "Language and Race." In *Routledge Companion to the Philosophy of Language,* edited by Russell, Gillian and Delia Graff Fara, 753–67. New York: Routledge, 2012.

Levine, Sam and Ankita Rao. "In 2013 the Supreme Court Gutted Voting Rights—how has it Changed the US?" *The Guardian,* June 25, 2020. http://www.theguardian.com/us-news/2020/jun/25/shelby-county-anniversary-voting-rights-act-consequences.

Lewis, Colin J. and Jennifer Kling. "Justified Revolution in Contemporary American Democracy: A Confucian-Inspired Account." In *The Crisis of American*

Democracy: Essays on a Failing Institution, edited by Leland Harper, 167–92. Wilmington, DE: Vernon Press, 2022.

Lewis, Heidi R., Dana Maria Asbury, and Jazlyn Andrews. *In Audre's Footsteps: Transnational Kitchen Table Talk*. Berlin: edition assemblage, 2021. https://www .barnesandnoble.com/w/in-audres-footsteps-heidi-r-lewis/1140303869.

Li, David K. "Charge Dropped Against White Woman Who Called Police on Black Bird-Watcher." *NBC News*, February 16, 2021. https://www.nbcnews.com/news/us-news/ charge-dropped-against-white-woman-who-called-police-black-n1257987.

Livingston, Alexander. "The Cost of Liberty: Sacrifice and Survival in Du Bois's John Brown." In *A Political Companion to W.E.B. Du Bois*, edited by Bromell, Nick, 207–40. Lexington: University Press of Kentucky, 2018.

Lorde, Audre. "Age, Race, Class, and Sex: Women Redefining Difference." In *Sister Outsider*. Berkeley, CA: Crossing Press, 2007.

———. "The Transformation of Silence." In *Sister Outsider*. Berkeley, CA: Crossing Press, 2007.

Malcolm X and Alex Haley. *The Autobiography of Malcolm X: As Told to Alex Haley*. New York: Ballantine Books, 1992.

McBride, David. *Caring for Equality: A History of African American Health and Healthcare*. Lanham, MD: Rowman & Littlefield, 2018.

McIntosh, Kriston, Emily Moss, Ryan Nunn, and Jay Shambaugh. "Examining the Black-White Wealth Gap." *Brookings*, February 27, 2020. https://www.brookings .edu/blog/up-front/2020/02/27/examining-the-Black-white-wealth-gap/.

McKinnon, Rachel. "Epistemic Injustice." *Philosophy Compass* 11, no. 8 (2016): 437–46.

Mills, Charles W. *The Racial Contract*. Ithaca, NY: Cornell University Press, 1997.

Mitchell, Megan. ""White People, we Need to Stop being so Damn Fragile!": White and Male Fragility as Epistemic Arrogance." In *Pacifism, Politics, and Feminism: Intersections and Innovations*, edited by Jennifer Kling, 51–67. Netherlands: Brill Rodopi, 2019.

Nagesh, Ashitha. "What Exactly is a 'Karen' and Where did the Meme Come from?" *BBC*, July 31, 2020. https://www.bbc.com/news/world-53588201.

Oluo, Ijeoma. *So You Want to Talk about Race*. First ed. New York, NY: Seal Press, 2018.

Oxley, Deborah. "'The Seat of Death and Terror': Urbanization, Stunting, and Small-pox." *The Economic History Review* 56, no. 4 (2003): 623–56. http://www.jstor .org/stable/3698721.

Parker, Ned, Linda So, Brad Heath, and Grant Smith. "Spread of Corona-virus Accelerates in U.S. Jails and Prisons." *Reuters*, March 28, 2020. https://www.reuters.com/article/us-health-coronavirus-usa-inmates-insigh/ spread-of-coronavirus-accelerates-in-us-jails-and-prisons-idUSKBN21F0TM.

Plato. *Meno*. Translated by Jowett, Benjamin. Champaign, Ill: Project Gutenberg, 1990.

Popovic, Srdja. *Blueprint for Revolution: How to use Rice Pudding, Lego Men, and Other Nonviolent Techniques to Galvanize Communities, Overthrow Dictators, Or Simply Change the World*. New York: Spiegel & Grau, 2015.

Rawls, John. *A Theory of Justice, Revised Edition.* Cambridge, MA: Belknap Press, 1999.

Rorty, Richard. "Religion as Conversation-Stopper." *Common Knowledge* 3, no. 1 (1994): 1–6.

1776 Commission Takes Historic and Scholarly Step to Restore Understanding of the Greatness of the American Founding. Washington, DC: The White House, 2021.

Severe, Sal. *How to Behave so Your Children Will, Too!* New York: Penguin Books, 2003.

Silverman, Hollie. "Coronavirus is Tearing through Prison and Jail Populations in Ohio and Illinois." *CNN,* April 20, 2020. https://www.cnn.com/2020/04/20/us/coronavirus-in-prisons-illinois-ohio/index.html.

Sinclair, Upton. *I, Candidate for Governor: And how I Got Licked.* Berkeley: University of California Press, 1934.

Staff. "Khmer Rouge: Cambodia's Years of Brutality." *BBC,* November 16, 2018. https://www.bbc.com/news/world-asia-pacific-10684399.

Steinmetz-Jenkins, Daniel. "Charles Mills Thinks Liberalism Still has a Chance." *The Nation,* January 28, 2021. https://www.thenation.com/article/culture/charles-mills-thinks-theres-still-time-to-rescue-liberalism/.

Strickland, Patrick. "US Anti-Fascists: 'We can make Racists Afraid again'." *Al Jazeera,* February 21, 2017. https://www.aljazeera.com/features/2017/2/21/us-anti-fascists-we-can-make-racists-afraid-again.

Swartzer, Steven. "Punishment and Democratic Rights: A Case Study in Non-Ideal Penal Theory." In *The Ethics of Policing and Imprisonment,* edited by Molly Gardner and Michael Weber, 7–37. New York: Palgrave Macmillan, 2018.

Swartzer, Steven. "Traumatic Incarceration." Unpublished Paper. Presented at RoME XII: Boulder, CO, 2019.

Tatum, Beverly Daniel. *Why are all the Black Kids Sitting Together in the Cafeteria? and Other Conversations about Race.* New York: Perseus Books, 1997.

Theoharis, Jeanne. *A More Beautiful and Terrible History: The Uses and Misuses of Civil Rights History.* Boston, MA: Beacon Press, 2018.

Thom, Shelby and Darrian Matassa-Fung. "'Disgusting' Halloween Display Featuring Confederate Flag and Noose Haunts Kelowna Resident." *Global News,* October 27, 2021. https://globalnews.ca/news/8330322/disgusting-halloween-display-confederate-flag-noose/.

Uggen, Christopher, Ryan Larson, and Sarah Shannon. "6 Million Lost Voters: State-Level Estimates of Felony Disenfranchisement, 2016." *The Sentencing Project,* October 6, 2016. https://www.sentencingproject.org/publications/6-million-lost-voters-state-level-estimates-felony-disenfranchisement-2016/.

Uggen, Christopher, Sarah Shannon, and Jeff Manza. *State-Level Estimates of Felon Disenfranchisement in the United States, 2010.* The Sentencing Project: Washington, DC, 2012.

Walker, Samuel and Charles Katz. *The Police in America: An Introduction.* 8th ed. New York: McGraw-Hill, 2012.

Wallace, Danielle. "Chicago Jail Becomes Top Coronavirus Hot Spot, Exceeding Cases Aboard USS Roosevelt." *Fox News,* April 9, 2020. https://www.foxnews.com/us/chicago-jail-coronavirus-hotspot-uss-roosevelt.

Wamsley, Laurel. "MacKenzie Scott has Donated More than $4 Billion in Last 4 Months." *NPR,* December 16, 2020. https://www.npr.org/2020/12/16/947189767/mackenzie-scott-has-donated-more-than-4-billion-in-last-4-months.

Waxman, Olivia B. "How the U.S. Got its Police Force." *Time*, May 18, 2017. https://time.com/4779112/police-history-origins/.

"What Smokey Robinson, Matthew McConaughey and More Stars are Saying about COVID-19." *USA Today,* updated November 26, 2021. https://www.usatoday.com/picture-gallery/entertainment/celebrities/2020/03/18/coronavirus-stars-tom-hanks-taylor-swift-idris-elba-ariana-grande-lady-gaga-reactions/5072632002/.

White, Gillian B. "There are Currently 4 Black CEOs in the Fortune 500." *The Atlantic*, October 26, 2017.

Williams, Timothy and Danielle Ivory. "Chicago's Jail is Top U.S. Hot Spot as Virus Spreads Behind Bars." *New York Times,* April 8, 2020. https://www.nytimes.com/2020/04/08/us/coronavirus-cook-county-jail-chicago.html.

Wilson, Yolonda. "A Time for Grief, not 'Resilience.'" *Daily Nous,* November 22, 2021. https://dailynous.com/2021/11/22/philosophers-on-how-the-pandemic-has-changed-us/?fbclid=IwAR2S7WUoZxrdJ0nA-vci7YYKvPB8TUkSAYrziSGreh3XC5HTg4i49kZfJPA#wilson.

Yancy, George. *Backlash: What Happens when we Talk Honestly about Racism in America*. Lanham, MD: Rowman & Littlefield, 2018.

———. *Black Bodies, White Gazes: The Continuing Significance of Race in America*. Second Edition. Lanham, MD: Rowman & Littlefield, 2017.

———. "Dear White America." *New York Times,* December 24, 2015. https://opinionator.blogs.nytimes.com/2015/12/24/dear-white-america/.

Young, Iris Marion. *Justice and the Politics of Difference*. Princeton, NJ: Princeton University Press, 1990.

———. *Responsibility for Justice*. Oxford: Oxford University Press, 2011.

Zack, Naomi. *The American Tragedy of COVID-19: Social and Political Crises of 2020*. Lanham, MD: Rowman & Littlefield, 2021.

Zheng, Robin. "What Kind of Responsibility do we have for Fighting Injustice? A Moral-Theoretic Perspective on the Social Connections Model." *Critical Horizons* 20, no. 2 (2019): 109–26. DOI: 10.1080/14409917.2019.1596202.

Index

About the Authors

Leland Harper is associate professor of philosophy at Siena Heights University. His research focuses on philosophy of religion and philosophy of race, particularly issues in miracles and religious experience, deism, racial solidarity, and racism. He is the author of *Multiverse Deism: Shifting Perspectives of God and the World* (2020), as well as articles in *Res Philosophica*, *Global Discourse: An Interdisciplinary Journal of Current Affairs*, *Humanities Bulletin*, *Forum Philosophicum*, the *International Journal of Philosophy and Theology*, and several edited volumes. He is also the editor of *The Crisis of American Democracy: Essays on a Failing Institution* (2022) and is the editor of the Philosophy of Race series at Vernon Press. He is the organizer of the Great Lakes Philosophy Conference, an annual international philosophy conference hosted by Siena Heights University. Leland grew up in Vancouver, British Columbia, and received a BA in general studies from Kwantlen Polytechnic University, an MA in philosophy from Ryerson University (though this university is currently undergoing a name change to Toronto Metropolitan University as part of its process of truth and reconciliation), and a PhD in philosophy from the University of Birmingham. In his spare time, he operates Leland Harper Consulting, a diversity, equity, and inclusion consulting firm based in Toronto, spends time with his wife and two children, and can be found cheering on the Boston Red Sox and the Los Angeles Clippers.

Jennifer Kling is assistant professor of philosophy and director of the Center for Legal Studies at the University of Colorado, Colorado Springs. Her research focuses on moral and political philosophy, particularly issues in war and peace, self- and other-defense, international relations, protest, philosophy of race, and feminism. She is the author of *War Refugees: Risk, Justice, and Moral Responsibility* (2019) and coauthor of *The Philosophy of Protest:*

Fighting for Justice Without Going to War (with Megan Mitchell, 2021). She has also authored articles in *Radical Philosophy Review, Res Philosophica, Journal of Global Ethics,* the *Routledge Handbook of Pacifism and Non-violence,* several edited volumes, and is the editor of *Pacifism, Politics, and Feminism: Intersections and Innovations* (2019). She is also the executive director of Concerned Philosophers for Peace, the largest and most active organization of professional philosophers in North America involved in the analysis of the causes of war and prospects for peace. Jennifer grew up in Indiana and received a BA in English and philosophy from the University of North Carolina at Chapel Hill, an MA in philosophy from the University of Colorado at Boulder, and a PhD in philosophy from the University of North Carolina at Chapel Hill. In her spare time, she practices the sport of Olympic fencing and does aerial fabrics, takes her husky on long hikes, and is hope-lessly addicted to skittles.

CPSIA information can be obtained
at www.ICGtesting.com
Printed in the USA
LVHW071804160623
749772LV00043B/16

9 781793 640420